SAVVy
Communication Skills for Family Members and Friends of Those with Borderline Personality Disorder

Karyn Hall

Contributors: Jim Hall, Diane Hall,

Tami Green, Samantha Bingham, and

Amanda Wang

ISBN: 10- 0615965938
ISBN-13: 978-0615965932

DEDICATION

For Jim and Diane Hall, who have helped so many with their wisdom and generosity.

CONTENTS

ACKNOWLEDGMENTS

My sincere thanks to Jim and Diane Hall, Tami Green, Samantha Bingham and Amanda Wang. Their courage and knowledge amazes me. My thanks to the DBT team members in Houston and to all the clients who have taught me about borderline personality disorder and emotional sensitivity. My thanks to Marsha Linehan, Ph.D. for creating Dialectical Behavior Therapy.

INTRODUCTION

Many individuals and their families and friends have been down a long, bumpy road before getting diagnosis of Borderline Personality Disorder (BPD). Many are frustrated with the difficulty in obtaining an accurate diagnosis, effective treatment or finding clinicians who offer helpful guidance to families. Parents, friends and spouses often feel they are in the dark about the right way to offer support and help.

When someone you love has Borderline Personality Disorder (BPD) or difficulty regulating their emotions, it's hard to understand their reactions because they can be so different from your own and most people you know. When your friend calls you at work for the tenth time, crying because her boyfriend is going on a business trip and she's sure she's lost the relationship forever, it's likely that her experience doesn't make sense to you. Even though you love her, her behavior is annoying. You may hesitate to tell her though because you fear her reaction. In fact, you find that you dread hearing from her when she is emotionally upset and want to avoid upsetting her if at all possible. When she's in a good mood though, she's so much fun and she's always the one to make life more interesting.

There are two main goals of this book. Only two, but they're big ones. The first is to explain what it feels like to not be able to regulate your emotion regulations. I hope you'll understand as much as possible what emotion dysregulation feels like to the person who has BPD. Though you don't have to understand the disorder to be able to communicate effectively and support someone with difficult to manage emotions, it is easier if you do. Samantha Bingman and Amanda Wang, who have emotion regulation disorder, share their experiences in a vivid way to help you walk a bit in their shoes. In addition, Jim and Diane Hall will give a family perspective of the symptoms—what it is like to have family members with the disorder (Chapter 16). They will also share how they overcame their own shame and guilt in order to move forward. Many families struggle with blaming themselves, sometimes to the point that they avoid getting help and support. Jim and Diane will offer hope and relief to many by sharing their journey.

The second goal is to provide you with skills for interacting with someone who has an emotion dysregulation disorder. I've called the skills SAVVy. SAVVy stands for Support, Appreciate, Validate and Love Your Family and Friends with BPD. I want to help you become SAVVy parents, SAVVy spouses, SAVVy siblings, and SAVVy friends. Recovery for consumers will be enhanced by having knowledgeable, SAVVy people who support them.

The second goal, learning skills for effective communication and support, depends on the first-- understanding. Having understanding gives you a foundation for the skills we offer in SAVVy.

SAVVy is an advanced communication program. We encourage you to participate in Family Connections, offered through the National Education Alliance for Borderline Personality Disorder before learning SAVVy. SAVVy builds on many of the skills that are taught in those classes. In addition, the sharing among families and friends and the in person learning format is invaluable.

SAVVy is based on Dialectical Behavior Therapy, developed by Marsha Linehan, Ph.D. As a DBT therapist, the concepts I've described in this book are based on DBT. I've made an attempt to apply her work for use by family members and friends. Many of the ideas are based on the genius of Marsha Linehan.

Recovery is possible. Marsha Linehan, Ph.D., the treatment developer of Dialectical Behavior Therapy, is one example of recovery. And there are many others. Tami Green, an amazing woman who learned to regulate her intense emotions shares her story of recovery in Chapter 17. Learning skills to manage your own emotions and interactions effectively is the best step you can take to support your loved one in their recovery.

2   UNDERSTANDING BORDERLINE PERSONALITY DISORDER

Many times people with BPD go from specialist to specialist receiving multiple diagnoses. Because they rotate through different self-damaging behaviors to manage their intense emotional pain they have often been diagnosed with substance abuse or an eating disorder or other addiction problem. Whatever behavior is being used to numb their intense feelings must be treated, but the person with intense emotions will most likely turn to another behavior to numb their feelings if they don't learn healthy ways to cope.

Dr. Marsha Linehan has proposed that Borderline Personality Disorder (BPD) be renamed to Emotion Regulation Disorder (ERD). Emotion Regulation Disorder is not in The Diagnostic and Statistical Manual of Mental Disorders (DSM V), the book that gives the criteria used by mental health professionals to make diagnoses. However, in my experience ERD more accurately reflects the issues that individuals struggle with who have intense emotions. Dr. Linehan (1993) suggests five different areas of dysregulation: Emotion Dysregulation, Behavioral Dysregulation, Interpersonal Dysregulation, Self-Dysregulation and Cognitive Dysregulation.

Emotion Dysregulation

Emotion dysregulation means not managing emotions effectively. It means that the person is reacts more frequently and faster to emotional events, her emotions are more intense and that she takes longer to calm than most other people do. Maybe she has intense rage, anxiety, irritability or depression, for example, to events that wouldn't upset others and her emotions interfere with her daily functioning--that would be emotion dysregulation.

Individuals with BPD have very intense feelings and that includes anger. Intense anger is quite difficult for people who love the person with BPD as the way the anger is expressed is usually destructive and almost always uncomfortable for those around them. For those who express their anger in rages or aggressive episodes, feelings of shame may follow, adding to the problem with regulating emotions. Mavis's behavior is an example of this cycle.

Mavis is a forty-year-old mother of two young daughters. For months, Mavis wanted to be part of a religious group that offers membership by invitation only. She belittled and put herself down as not being worthy of the group. When she finally received an invitation to participate in a seminar with that religious group, she became so anxious, she wondered if she should even go. She doubted that she would be able to overcome her fears. By the evening she felt depressed, believing no one at the group would like her or that she wouldn't be able to talk to anyone. The next day she felt angry that the group was so exclusive and snooty and decided she didn't want to belong. She declined their invitation

Individuals with emotional regulation disorder often act in unpredictable ways as a result of their emotional reactivity and poor impulse control. Their unpredictability can keep you off balance. Family members and friends rarely know what to expect and as a result are often hyper alert and on guard. Some days your loved one is able to laugh at the same comment that enrages her on another day. Sometimes she is upset, saying that you hate her or are criticizing her when you did not intend either. Sometimes her fears of what might happen lead her to act as if the feared event did or will happen, though it hasn't. Jancey, whose spouse is completely committed to their marriage, once expressed, "I know he's going to leave me, so I asked for a divorce so I can leave him first." That can be confusing.

From the outside the behavior of the individual with BPD often doesn't make sense. You see how they could have so much less suffering if they would just stop getting so upset or stop taking comments so personally or get a job or go make friends. While those tasks might appear easy to most, individuals with BPD have a constant struggle with intense emotions that make everyday life difficult. They often feel like a small rowboat being tossed about in an ocean storm with no port or anchor. One day the world is fabulous and the next, or even a few hours later, all is miserable. The person's mood tends to be situation-dependent and sometimes person-dependent. She does not understand how to just let something go or overlook the small stuff because to her there is no small stuff. To use a different analogy, she is like a third degree burn victim walking around in a world raining porcupine quills.

Over time you may become impatient and have the "here we go again" reaction when observing your loved one's mood. You may stop including the person you love with BPD in certain events. You may become estranged after too many ruined celebrations and get-togethers. Some family members or friends may become angry at the special treatment they believe the individual with BPD is getting.

Behavioral Dysregulation

Behavioral dysregulation is characterized by self-injury and impulsive behaviors (such as substance abuse, promiscuity, excessive shopping). This means engaging in self-damaging behavior without thinking of the consequences. The behavior of individuals with BPD is driven by emotion. Their self-harm behavior often is an effort to numb or relieve intensely painful feelings.

Hillary, 37 years old, lives with her husband. She has been hospitalized over thirty times, starting when she was 18. She seemed to rotate through substance abuse, reckless driving, overspending, sexual acting out, cutting, and bulimia. When she first saw a new therapist five years ago she was addicted to crystal meth. She detoxed successfully, stayed sober, but then began throwing up after meals. Because of her past history of an eating disorder, her health was seriously threatened when she lost down to a weight of 105 pounds, at a height of 5'9. She recovered from the anorexia but began drinking too much. She attended AA meetings and began sleeping with several of the men who attended the meetings. Her behaviors didn't fill her emptiness and she felt more miserable and suicidal after each episode. As illogical as her behavior might seem, she was doing her best to stop the emotional pain she felt. Numbing in various ways were the only ways she knew to do that.

Repeated suicide gestures, threats or behaviors is one of the most difficult symptoms for therapists and families alike. Rosa made her first suicide attempt when she was 12 and her parents divorced. Her father remarried a woman with children of her own then moved to another state. Rosa felt like her father had replaced her and didn't need her anymore. She made another attempt at 17, when her boyfriend broke up with her. She pleaded and begged for him to return and then threatened to kill herself if he didn't. When he told her he had a new girlfriend, she made a suicide attempt. She is now 35 and has made 14 attempts. A number of therapists have terminated treatment because of her suicide attempts.

For some people with BPD, suicidal threats and attempts are ways they attempt to solve problems. Sometimes those actions are the only way they know to get others to listen to them, to get their needs met, to communicate how much pain they are in, to avoid abandonment or to relieve their pain and suffering. Some are acting impulsively, but in that moment they are sure they want to die and they act on that feeling. Others may have struggled with pain for a long time and may feel overwhelmed and tired. Self-mutilation helps ease the emotional pain that people with BPD experience. Many people with BPD say they would rather cope with physical pain than emotional pain. There are many problems with using cutting or other self-harm behavior to cope with emotional pain, including stigma and sense of shame. Often it takes more extensive or deeper cutting to achieve the same numbing effect and the cuts gradually become more life threatening. Sometimes the superficial cuts may lead to more serious suicide attempts or the consumer misjudges and what was meant to be self-harm becomes lethal.

Self-Dysregulation

Self-dysregulation means not having a clear sense of your identity and experiencing a chronic sense of emptiness. Individuals with BPD may change their dress, speech, likes and dislikes and other characteristics to fit the group they are with or the view that they have of themselves at the time. Sometimes this identity includes self-destructive behavior, such as taking on the identity of an addict.

Janet had many husbands and many career starts. At 48 she had worked as a dance instructor, legal assistant, actress, insurance broker, physical therapist and Mary Kay saleswoman. She had married seven times and was having an affair at the time she entered therapy following a third serious suicide attempt. Janet reported that each time (except for one marriage) she was sure she had met the right man and had chosen the right career. Now she no longer trusted her decision-making. Her unstable identity made it difficult for her to be consistent in her profession as well as in her relationships.

People with BPD want to fill the emptiness inside as well as seek a way they won't be abandoned. They may alter their views, likes and dislikes and their personality style to please someone who is important to them. This includes their therapist. Sometimes the therapist gets an entirely different picture of the individual than the view of her parents, spouse, or frie Individuals who suffer from BPD may base their sense of self on their most recent experience. If they are turned down for a job, they are worthless. If a friend goes to lunch with someone else and doesn't invite them, then they have no friends. They are often not able to hold a general view of who they are.

One of the difficulties they have in learning who they are is that their emotions are so overwhelming there is no space to consider their identity. They are buffeted about with changing emotions and when they are not in the throes of emotion they judge themselves harshly for the way they behaved. Many want to be anyone but the person they believe themselves to be. They often do not see the many positive characteristics they have.

Everyone has a view of themselves, an understanding of who they are that has developed over time. You may see yourself as friendly, athletic, impatient, well-organized or good at math. If you have a belief that you are good at math and well-organized, then that affects how you interpret your experiences. If you receive an overdrawn notice from the bank, you are likely to believe that the bank made an error or that it was a fluke because you were traveling. You attribute the error to some reason outside yourself because it isn't like you. "I can't believe I did that," you might say. Then when the bank discovers that they made the error, you say, "I knew that couldn't have been my mistake."

On the other hand if your belief is that you are a disorganized person who is lousy at math, then you are likely to blame yourself whether it was your fault or not because it fits with how you see yourself. You may not let others know you blame yourself, particularly if you feel ashamed that you are disorganized or fearful that others will be upset with you. When you learn the bank made the error, you are relieved but it doesn't change how you see yourself. Most of the time our view of ourselves works well for us. We know we aren't good at sports, so we don't waste time trying every single sport repeatedly. As long as your view of yourself is based on facts, then it helps us make choices.

But what if the view you have of yourself isn't based on facts and isn't based on behavior and skills? Maybe your view of yourself is based on what you've been told by other people and those views are distorted. Many times the individual with BPD has a distorted view of herself that doesn't fit who she is but is a view that she believes without question. For example, imagine that you absolutely positively believe without a doubt that you are a bad mother. If someone says you are good mother, you will not believe them. You will tell yourself that they don't know the truth about you. You will only take in information that supports the basic belief you have about yourself. When you soothe your child or help him with his homework, that doesn't matter because you are sure you are a bad mother. When you hug your child and comfort him, celebrate his birthday, listen to his problems, encourage him when he feels low, you are still a bad mother. The problem is that you can't see the evidence that your belief about yourself isn't true. No evidence to the contrary can be taken in so the view stays the same regardless of how many people tell you differently.

Often individuals with BPD aren't mindful of positive experiences. When something positive happens, they may worry about the happiness ending or believe that they don't deserve happiness, or use any of a number of ways to distance themselves from the experience, all of which prevents taking in and fully experiencing the pleasant emotions. Feelings of shame and thoughts about not being worthy build walls against love and acceptance so they think others are lying when they say they care.

Individuals with BPD describe emptiness as a void in themselves, a kind of chronic boredom and lack of connection with others or the world. Sometimes it comes from being detached and not participating in life. For some it may be an inability to be mindful of and take in positive experiences and positive emotions, such as not being able to feel loved. For others it may be an inability to allow themselves to love others. Emptiness may be a lack of meaning in life or a lack of spirituality. Because the emptiness can be for different reasons, the perceived cause must be defined for each person.

Clara is a 23-year-old who recently moved into her own apartment following a stay in a residential treatment center. After the initial excitement of having her own place, Clara complained that she felt empty inside most of the time, especially at night. She tried to never be by herself. She chose one person to "mesh" with so she could feel part of that other person and let that person fill the emptiness. She would follow the lead of the chosen person until the relationship dissolved and then look for someone else.

Parents, friends and spouses are often amazed that their loved one with BPD feels empty. They ask, "How can he feel empty when I've done so much for him?" Unfortunately the emptiness can't be filled from the outside in. The ability to take in and hold onto the positive must be developed and so must an ability to remember the positive when something undesired occurs or when a problem can't be solved.

Interpersonal Dysregulation

Interpersonal dysregulation is indicated by chaotic relationships and fears of abandonment. The fear of being abandoned is terrifying for most people with BPD.

Mariah is a thirty-four-year old woman who has never lived away from home or held a job. She had completed three inpatient treatment programs and seen various psychiatrists. Disorganized in her behavior she took her meds sporadically and sometimes when in distress took more than prescribed, hoping to overcome her fears and avoid feeling sad. Under threat of being forced out of the home, she entered a day treatment program. At the recommendation of her new therapist, she allowed her mother to give her the medications as prescribed. In a week, she began to show progress in regulating her mood and in keeping her appointments. Her parents and her treatment team commented on her progress. Their comments about her progress triggered fears of being abandoned. If she got well what would happen to her relationship with her parents? The next week she refused to let her mother manage her medications and returned to taking them as she wanted. She stopped attending the day treatment program and stayed in her bedroom most of the day, threatening to harm herself if her mother did not stay in the house with her.

The fear of abandonment is one of the most difficult symptoms because getting well often means people with BPD must face the loss of attention and caretaking of loved ones. In fact one of the first actions people may take when the individual with BPD improves is to pull away, relieved. Many of the consumer's relationships may be centered around their being ill or in the role of a patient or someone who needs help. That may be the only way they have had relationships though the caretaker may have changed several times, such as multiple marriages or romantic partners. The pattern of losing relationships increases their fear of abandonment rather than leading them to change the way they interact.

The actions of people with BPD can be confusing because they often behave in ways that seem guaranteed to push loved ones away, when most of the time that's the last thing they truly want. That's because the person with BPD is thinking in the short term rather than the long term. They are using the best skills they know to get their needs met and to get reassurance that they are loved—in the short term. An example would be to behave in the very way that you hate the most in order to get you angry. That's proof that you still love them. If you get angry with them, then you still care. If you stop getting angry, they will try harder to provoke you so they can know you still care. Over time this anger may be the only way they have of connecting emotionally with you. In the short term, their needs are met. In the long run, the relationship is likely to be damaged and may not survive.

The fear of being abandoned exists inside of them and doesn't have to be (though it can be) triggered by any action or statement you make. Because this fear is part of their daily life, many times people with BPD will test others to see if they love them. One young man described it as follows: "I push my mother away to see if she loves me enough. If she begs me not be mad at her, then she cares about me. It doesn't matter if I did something to her or not. When she gets mad at me, I push her away even harder, to see if she cares about how I feel.

Someone with BPD may judge how much you care about them by how willing you are to meet their needs. They may define love as meaning that you say yes to what they want and that you are willing to drop everything when they ask for help. They may see your relationships with others as a threat to them and may set up situations in which you have to choose. Their behavior often comes form a desperate need to hold on to you, based on the fear of losing you. The fear cannot be explained away with logic or proven untrue, because for someone with BPD your love and devotion could change at any moment. Thus the testing continues regardless of how many "tests" are "passed." In fact, it is likely that the more you try to prove your love, the greater the demands made on you. Often they choose one person to focus their attachment on and thus also their fears of abandonment.

Some individuals with BPD handle their fears of abandonment differently. Instead of trying to hold on to relationships, they avoid having relationships. They prefer to live with the chronic pain of isolation than risk being abandoned and suffer those feelings of extreme loss. Sometimes they may alternate between isolating themselves from everyone and frantically attempting to prove to themselves that their parent or their spouse loves them.

Samantha explains what fears of abandonment are like for her:

Writing about abandonment is very hard; it brings up memories and feelings that many people, especially me, don't want to deal with. Having Borderline Personality Disorder I walk my daily life thinking and wondering when or who the next person will be that will disappoint me. In my world abandonment is not only when someone leaves you, it is when someone disappoints you, when they leave you out of a conversation, when you get left out of a vacation, and a number of other ways. Whenever I feel abandoned I feel numb, frozen, and paralyzed in my own existence. I think it hurts inside so bad, when it feels like someone doesn't like you or that someone is going away, because you automatically think you have done something wrong. Your mind does terrible things and goes down this path of what did I do? Why am I such a horrible person? Why do bad things always happen to me? It's easier to not feel then feel anything at all or have your mind go down that awful rabbit trail.

I find myself pushing people away and keeping them at a specific distance because I am afraid they will leave and I would rather not get hurt, or I would rather it not hurt so bad when they do leave. The feeling of abandonment is so intense, I live my life avoiding love/closeness and pretending it doesn't exist. The paradox of it all is that I don't want to feel alone then the fear of abandonment ignites, I then shut my heart down and put up my guard allowing myself to not be vulnerable which then still leaves me alone.

Idealization and Devaluation

Most relationships vacillate with varying periods of closeness, conflict, and distance over time. For the person with BPD, relationships are often dramatic and involve intense swings from thinking you are the best person in the world (idealization) to your being the worst human being in the world (devaluation). This is sometimes referred to as black and white thinking. Sometimes you may not even know the reason for the change in the way you are viewed.

John felt grateful when he got a job as an apprentice, working for Andrew, a well-known photographer in his city. He looked up to Andrew and worked hard to learn what Andrew could teach. He told everyone how lucky he was to work with Andrew. When a local celebrity wanted several photographers to cover her wedding, John felt sure he would be one of them, but Andrew told him he wasn't ready. John devalued Andrew, decided Andrew was jealous of his work and wanted to keep him as an assistant to control him. Furious, John told everyone in the business how controlling Andrew was. He encouraged other employees to quit. Finally Andrew fired John, which only made John more angry.

When someone idealizes you, sees you as the only person who understands, the only one who can help through the difficult times, the only one she really trusts, that can be a big responsibility. Whether you are a therapist or a family member being thought of so highly may bring out a wish to not let the person down, not disappoint her and to "save" her. Often the idealized people in this situation also believe that they are the only ones who understand the person with BPD and that they can make her life different. That is, if they haven't experienced idealization before. For those who have been through it, they know that devaluation follows idealization. Even if the person makes correct and reasonable decisions there will come a point when they are devalued, because they will not be able to take away the pain the consumer feels.

One of the situations that family members face is the idealization and devaluation of treatment providers. Some people with BPD move from therapist to therapist. Sometimes they leave saying the therapist was inept and incompetent. Not all therapists know how to work effectively with BPD, so finding a therapist who specializes with BPD is important. However even when the therapist is a specialist, some consumers go in and out of therapy and repeatedly change therapists, and thus their pattern of unstable relationships makes it difficult to have a working relationship with a therapist as well. There can be many reasons. Perhaps they become disappointed when the therapist can't make their problems disappear. It is possible they are viewing the therapist through the eyes of disappointment. They may see the new therapist with hope and not see any faults or weaknesses that could damage that hope. Or maybe focusing on issues was too painful for them. In their personal life they may have the same cycle of idealizing and devaluing which makes it difficult to keep friends.

"In my life, relationships are like rubber bands. They stretch and snap back so many times, but eventually something breaks and there's no way to repair the damage" (Van Gelder, 2010). Individuals with BPD glamourize and vilify, sometimes based on an interaction occurring at the moment. You may be the most wonderful person on earth until you say no to something, then you are the worst person on earth. This creates a revolving door of relationships and/or a rollercoaster of ups and downs that wears family members out. One result is that loved ones come to fear being devalued and go to unreasonable lengths to avoid it.

The lack of consistency in relationships contributes to the feelings of abandonment for the person with BPD. Despite it often being their choice to leave a relationship, the person with borderline personality disorder still sees herself as repeatedly abandoned. If someone is angry with her, she may see that as abandonment as well. Someone saying no to an invitation may be seen by some as abandonment. This is often not logical and not based on facts. But feelings are not necessarily based on facts and this is the way the consumer feels. Often the person with BPD believes that what she feels is true, so if she feels abandoned, then she must be abandoned. That is a painful experience.

Many times individuals with BPD, when emotionally upset, have limited empathy for other people and focus on whether their own needs are being met. Portia, a 22 year old, was usually considerate and caring about her mother who worked eighty-hour weeks during a take over for her company. But when she was upset, she yelled and screamed that her mother wasn't supporting her in her treatment, though Portia rarely kept her appointments. When emotionally upset, Portia felt abandoned by her mother and wasn't able to allow the many demands on her mother to mitigate those feelings. At that moment she couldn't see how her behavior affected her mother.

Another reason relationships are unstable is that individuals with BPD have difficulty holding onto good feelings. It is almost like every day or even every hour the relationship starts over and all the positive interactions of the past disappear. So even though you have stuck by your daughter through many difficult situations, if you refuse to take her to the airport, then you don't love her. If you are angry that she wrecked your car for the tenth time, you are abandoning her. She believes that if you love her you will meet her needs and if you don't, then you are horrible. To you, this may seem unreasonable. If you can imagine what it is like to only be able to value the relationship in terms of what has just occurred, you may be able to understand better.

Idealization and devaluation are big girl terms. My mom likes to call it my alter ego is coming out or the people at work have named me Heather. I have this boss that I have this love and hate relationship with. I go to her when I am really sad because I think very highly of her and she is important to me yet when she doesn't respond to my text message right away I "cut her off" and pretend to be mad at her. I am generally really nice and outgoing on my own then "Heather" is nice and outgoing with an attitude and lots of spunk.

In a borderline's world most things are black and white but when it comes to relationships they are really black and white. For instance I love my mom at the beginning of the conversation but by the end of a conversation because she said she took my sister to get her nails done and didn't take me I hate her. She is the worst person ever and I can't stand her. I will find every little thing that is wrong with her and point it out and throw it right in her face. I think the only reason you would attack someone so hard is to keep yourself from feeling the initial pain, i.e., I was left out ("abandoned").

It is my honest opinion that borderlines do not like to feel. I know that I

14

don't like to feel anything. I thought for a long time that it was because I didn't know how to feel but really it's because I just don't like to feel. Because I don't like to feel anything I use any defense mechanism that is convenient. All idealization and devaluation is, is a defense mechanism for when you feel pain.

Another example I can think about is that the one dog I loved died and left me, therefore I hate dogs. I don't like pets in general. I also think some people are perfect and when I find out they are not perfect I am disappointed time and time again because I have this false belief that they have no flaws and could possible do no wrong. It is so hard to have an interpersonal relationship when you constantly have this I hate you don't leave me mentality or are completely up and down all the time

In the beginning of a therapy relationship, individuals with BPD may hope the therapist can fill the horrible emptiness they feel, as they know of no way to fill it themselves. Often after a cautious beginning, they begin to lean on the therapist and turn to him for rescue from the emotional pain and chaos, knowing what he will respond to. The therapist may have promised that he would never abandon the client. Therapists usually respond to emergency calls and most all dysfunctional behavior with increased concern and attention. Instead of getting better, the BPD client needs more and more, trying to fill the emptiness inside and get relief from the pain. Unfortunately the therapist, with the best of intentions, expects that the client will improve as a result of the increased support and attention. When that doesn't happen, the therapist begins to tire and sometimes becomes hopeless. The therapist withdraws and may decide to transfer the client. The client then feels more hopeless and empty than before.

Spouses, parents and other loved ones may have the same experience. They may expend significant energy and resources to reassure the individual with BPD and to help her feel loved and full. When their efforts do not work in the long run they too may feel hopeless. Individuals with BPD become more hopeless when others withdraw or give up.

Because individuals with BPD don't have a solid identity, they can't feel loved for themselves. Others don't really know them, so how can they say they love them? At the same time they are afraid to show who they are because they believe others won't accept them. So it's a cycle of putting on a mask out of fear of rejection and then not feeling truly loved because they aren't being themselves. Most have had the repeated experience of people leaving them because of their symptoms. It's difficult to have stable relationships with these issues. In fact, we know that interpersonal relationship difficulties are the behaviors that seem to persist the longest when the individual recovering.

Liz loved her family but whenever any of them did something she didn't approve of she raged at them. She believed if they loved her they would do what she said. When they didn't do what she thought best, she felt rejected as well as terrified that their lives would be ruined. She withdrew, refused to talk with them, and created so much tension that no one felt comfortable in the house with her. She would threaten to leave and sometimes did. For example, Kylie, her nineteen-year-old daughter, wanted her father to take her camping. Liz doesn't enjoy camping, but didn't want Kylie to go with her Dad. She felt they were pushing her out and that her husband was playing the good guy and making her look bad. Liz didn't express her fears. Instead she withdrew and made plans of her own to go away that weekend. She told her therapist she'd had enough of their games and she was going to have some fun on her own.

The intense anger that individuals with Borderline Personality Disorder sometimes have can also interfere with relationships. Others fear triggering their anger. Sometimes their anger is their primary way to get their needs met and sometimes their anger is the way emotional dysregulation is expressed. They may display anger when they are hurt or sad or feeling vulnerable in any way. Sometimes anger is less scary and feels more protective than the other emotions. Their anger may be directed at others or expressed through harm to themselves. For example, one woman said about her sister who she lived with, "I want her to wake up every morning and know it was her fault I killed myself. " One husband who suffered from BPD said to his wife, "Why don't you spend your day thinking about what color lining to put in my coffin? Just know that you're the one who killed me."

Cognitive Dysregulation

Cognitive dysregulation is indicated by distortions, suspiciousness and dissociative responses. Dissociative symptoms include derealisation and depersonalization and involve an interruption of awake consciousness. Depersonalization is a feeling of being disconnected from your body or that your body doesn't belong to you. Derealisation means feeling disconnected from the world. "Spacing out" is a form of derealisation. Dissociative symptoms are thought to be coping mechanisms -- the person literally dissociates himself from a situation or experience too traumatic to deal with. Stress makes these responses worse.

One of the key ingredients for effective therapy is a healthy relationship and a healthy relationship is based on trust. Clients with BPD become highly suspicious of others easily. They may distort what others say to fit their fears. Dissociation means they separate the mind or awareness from the emotions and/or the body. Dissociation can be mild, such as you experience when you drive home and have no idea how you got there. It can be more severe, such as dissociating to the point they aren't really aware of what is happening around them and won't remember interactions that occur or statements made. This reaction stresses relationships and can be frightening to the consumer and the family.

Overview of the BPD Experience: Amanda Wang

Amanda Wang is in recovery from BPD. She describes a day in her life of struggling with the disorder.

What will it take for me to kill myself today?

It was the one constant question in my head. An ordinary commute to and from the office became a minefield strewn with opportunities to die: the belt I wore around my waist, subway tracks (and more specifically the oncoming train), crossing the busy New York City streets on a green light, even the police officers standing guard at the train station. All became doors desperately waiting to be flung open; all in hopes of closing the gate on a life I failed to identify or connect with.

Suicide and self-injury. Perhaps two of the most notoriously misunderstood and forever linked behaviors of mental illness, and more specifically, borderline personality disorder. I have come to my own personal understanding about the difference between these two hallmark symptoms. Trailing off where the other begins, they work in tangent as seductive problem solvers for a immediate and quick fix. One is the desire to end unbearable suffering; the other the desire to make suffering bearable again.

Oftentimes suicide attempts and self-injury are the only clear signs that something has gone awry. Many who have lived through it will tell you, however, that these distinct behaviors are symptoms of a more deeply rooted issue.

> *Today I feel worthless. It's not*
> *the first time I've contemplated*
> *life better off without me*
> *because really, what is a person*
> *with mental illness actually good*
> *for? They bring everybody*
> *down. They can't think of anyone*
> *but themselves. They just take up*
> *space, nothing of substance. No*
> *drive. No soul. No life. Today I*
> *want to disappear and maybe*
> *everyone will be happier if i*
> *didn't exist.*

Clinicians technically call this *identity disturbance* or *identity incoherence*. It is the crux of my BPD, torturing my psyche with a constant dilemma: do I cede to the incessant voices of unworthiness or do I continue my hopeless efforts to prove what I am worth? Living in this cloud of extreme thinking has set me up for a perfect storm of failure.

This incoherence — my inability to integrate the fact that who I am can find a home somewhere around these paradigms instead of at odds with them — put me between a rock and a hard place. I lived a psychiatric battle of epic proportions on a day-to-day, hour-by-hour basis.

I've lived much of my life like this, invalidating feelings of who I should and shouldn't be. Everything I experienced was compounded into a *why-it-can't-be, look-at-what's-wrong-with-you,* and *see-I-told-you-you're-no-good.*

Practice

I. Write the behaviors that your loved one shows that reflect BPD symptoms:

Fears of Abandonment

Suspiciousness

Changing Identity

Self-harm

Long term feelings of emptiness

Intense anger

Frequent mood changes

Impulsive behavior that is harmful

Recurrent suicidal thoughts or attempts

II. Now go back. Are there more behaviors that fit the symptoms? Be as thorough as possible, but also be specific to the symptom. If the behavior you are considering doesn't really fit any of the symptoms, leave it out for now.

III. Go back again. This time write your reactions to the symptoms. How does each affect you? How does your loved one react to your reactions?

Part 2

Knowing the symptoms gives you some ideas of what is helpful and what isn't. Any action or reaction that triggers dysregulation is likely to lead to emotion-driven, destructive behavior on the part of the individual with BPD. For example, threatening abandonment is not helpful. Not that you would say it that way, but any threat to leave the relationship is dysregulating. This doesn't mean that you can't set limits, but doing so in a particular way will be more effective. Adding to your loved one's already intense emotional state will not be helpful. Challenging or criticizing their identity, their internal views and feelings will increase dysregulation. Encouraging black and white views of people or supporting their views of people as all bad or all good is not helpful. Let's look at some examples and see if you can tell me what makes the behavior ineffective for interacting with someone with BPD.

Example 1: Jess, who is diagnosed with BPD and has never lived away from home, drops out of college for the second time. His parents meet him at the airport. Jess says he wants to go to San Francisco, get a job, and live close to his cousin A.J. His parents tell him that they will set him up in an apartment and help him get a job, but then he's on his own. They drive him to San Francisco, help him settle in an apartment and then his parents leave.

Example 2: Janice's parents give her a credit card to use in emergencies. She promises to use it only if her car breaks down, she needs urgent medical care, or for expenditures pre-approved by her parents. She has a monthly allowance to pay her rent and her bills. Though she has a history of excessive spending, she has kept this agreement for several months. Yesterday she learned that her boyfriend has cheated on her.

Example 3: Angela greets you at the door, excited to see you. She's made dinner and has tickets to go to the movies after dinner. She's telling you about her day, then remembers that the meatloaf is in the oven. She rushes to the kitchen but it is too late, the meatloaf is burned. She starts sobbing because her evening is ruined. She starts hitting her head with her fists saying she can't do anything right. You've been through this many times. You raise your voice slightly. "Why can't you just let it go? It's just meatloaf. We could still have a good evening if you didn't have to overreact."

Example 4: Lewis begins therapy with a new therapist. He is cautious but has hope the therapist can help him. At his third appointment his therapist tells him his wife called and the therapist summarizes the phone conversation in which his wife details the problems she sees Lewis having.

Example 5: Taylor is very grateful to you and her father for helping her get a new business started. She tells everyone how you are the perfect parents. She tells you how happy you have made her. After a few weeks in business she is disappointed in her sales. She wants to buy some commercial time on a shopping network and asks you to loan her additional money. She is sure she can make it big. You say no. She is crushed.

Example 6: Denise, who wears black and listens to alternative music, starts dating a young man who loves tattoos, rides a motorcycle and wears lots of leather. He listens to rock music.

Answers:

Example 1: Abandonment

Example 2: Impulsive behavior, Behaviors to numb emotions

Example 3: Intense emotions

Example 4: Paranoid Thoughts

Example 5: Devaluation

Example 6: Unstable Identity

3 DIALECTICAL THINKING

Marsha Linehan (1993) introduced the idea of dialectical thinking in the treatment of BPD. Dialectics means that two opposite views can both be true and can be used to come to a meaning that includes the truth of both views. Dialectical thinking also means that you recognize that you only have part of the truth and so you are open to what might be missing in your view of the world and other people. Dialectical thinking is the process especially associated with Hegel, a philosopher, of arriving at the truth by stating a thesis, developing a contradictory antithesis, and combining and resolving them into a coherent synthesis. Basically, that means that you have a belief, you consider the opposite belief, and you put the two together to come to a higher truth. It is not about compromising. It is about synthesis. It also means that you search for the truth in the other person's viewpoint instead of defending your own.

Dialectical thinking means considering the concept and its opposite or more specifically what an object or a concept is and what it is not. Think of figure and ground: everything has its contrast. An easy way of understanding this is with figure ground puzzles. What do you see in the picture below?

This is the Rubin vase/profile illusion. Many people see a vase. Others see two profiles. Which is right? Both are right. If you focus on the white space you will see a vase. If you focus on the black you will see the profiles of two people looking at each other.

Samantha gives an example of dialectics in her life, how she vacillates between two opposite ideas:

I go between being confident in myself or depending on all the time. I have always looked like I have everything going for myself and had myself all put together. I have this really great job, I have a really nice house, I pay all my bills on time, I am really responsible, I keep my house clean, I have a nice car that I pay for myself, all things that make my image for being so young. There is this part of me that so badly wants everyone to think that I am perfect and that I have everything all put together that I try so hard everyday. I eventually break and when I do I feel like the whole world knows that I can't do anything for myself. I feel like a small child again and I feel like I have to depend on everyone for everything. Sometimes it really isn't that bad but sometimes it is scary and I really feel like this little kid again and just want my mom. I depend on her to make all of my decisions because I am scared to do anything alone.

So both ideas are true. Sometimes she is independent and sometimes she is dependent. As with most of the characteristics of BPD, everyone has this experience. For someone with BPD it is more extreme.

Dialectics is helpful for family members and friends as well. In learning to communicate effectively with someone who has intense emotions, dialectical thinking allows you to see what you are missing, how someone else might view something differently, perhaps by focusing on a different emotion or a different thought or by having a different experience. When your wife is furious that you said no to her sister coming to live with you, her point of view might be that she is afraid she will lose her relationship with her sister. You may see that her sister creates chaos and upsets your wife, or that you don't have the finances to afford her staying with you. There is truth in both points of view. You don't have to give up your point of view to understand someone else's. If you understand the other person's point of view you can have a more effective discussion.

Guidelines For Dialectical Thinking

Look at what is missing. Consider all sides. One way to do this is to outline your point of view and the reasons you believe what you believe. Then consider the point of view of someone who has a different point of view. Think of the reasons they would have their point of view. Check the facts for both points of view.

Consider a way that both could be true, that neither view is right or wrong. Look for what is true in different views. If you are feeling indignant or outraged, you are not being dialectical. Being dialectical means you realize there is always another point of view and that no one has all the knowledge possible, particularly when it involves what is important to another person.

Instead of exclusion or black and white thinking, which is usually either/or, think inclusively. Inclusive thinking usually uses words like both/and/sometimes/.

Examples: You always yell at me. *What is being left out? The times when the person listens calmly plus the times when they laugh together.*

Dialectical thinking would be: Sometimes you yell at me and sometimes you are kind and gentle.

Sometimes the other person's truth may be difficult to grasp. Sometimes you may need to look hard to uncover the truth in what they are saying. Maybe there is a small truth that is at the core but it may be difficult to see because of other statements that do not seem logical or accurate. Dr. Linehan (1993) calls this the "kernel of truth."

Practice Dialectical Thinking

Consider spring. Write all the things that you enjoy about spring. Now write the aspects of Spring that are not so desirable to you. You can also do winter and fall, favorite food, etc.

As you can see most everything has characteristics that we find desirable and some that we don't. Seeing the whole picture means we see both what we find desirable and what we don't, and what others may find desirable and not. The truth is in seeing both or as close as we can get to seeing both.

Choose the statement in the groups of three that represents dialectical thinking:

a. Nothing can help.

b. I may not get exactly the outcome I want and I can get relief.

c. This therapy will work in three or four sessions and my daughter will stop yelling at me.

a. I am always saying the wrong thing.

b. Sometimes I say interesting things and sometimes I say things that seem to upset others.

c. Other people are just too sensitive.

a. She's doing very well, I think we are through with the dysregulation.

b. She's always upset about something.

c. Most of the time she manages her emotions more effectively and sometimes she has difficulty with coping.

a. I can't stand it when she is upset.

b. I am used to her being upset, no problem.

c. Sometimes I use skills to effectively manage when I am worried and sometimes I still struggle.

a. We may not be able to travel as we wanted, and we can still have fun with friends and do activities in town.

b. We don't mind giving up our plans for our retirement.

c. There is no future for my husband and me anymore.

Think of an example of how you used dialectical thinking recently. How did it affect your mood?

A Dialectical View Of The Person You Love

The symptoms of BPD can take over your view of the person you love even though the person is so much more than the disorder. Keeping in perspective that the person has behaviors of BPD and is also more than those behaviors is important for your relationship. The following exercise is to help you keep in perspective what behaviors are results of the disorder and to remember the non-BPD personality characteristics of the person you love. In addition, clarifying what behaviors are reflective of BPD symptoms will help you cope with the situations when the disorder is causing difficulties. In this exercise, writing your responses is important. We hope you'll spend some time thinking about your answers and keep them so you can review them when you need to remember the person and not the illness.

Worksheet on Seeing Your Loved One Dialectically

Make a list of the personality characteristics that make your loved one who he is. Write as many characteristics you can think of. Try to not list symptoms that are a result of BPD or an emotion regulation disorder. Focus on positive personality characteristics, but include less desirable ones as well.

It's not always easy to be clear about what is a symptom of a disorder and what is not. For example, is anger always a characteristic of an emotional dysregulation disorder? Of course not. Anger is an emotion we are all born with and it serves a purpose. Intense angry episodes that are repeated and not justified and not effectively managed are characteristic of emotional dysregulation disorders. Sometimes it is easy to blame all the less than perfect qualities that someone has on their illness. Forgetting to pay a bill is something most everyone has done. Allowing your loved one to have emotions and make mistakes without it being blamed on the disorder is important.

Dialectical thinking means that you see the person and also the characteristics of the person that are not part of the illness. Being able to see the person separate from the disorder may seem like an abstract, perhaps impossible task. Perhaps it is frustrating because the disorder is so demanding. Though difficult, this task is worth the time and effort.

Seeing the person separate from the disorder may help you remember what is loveable about someone when they are frustrating to you. In addition, seeing your loved one's personality separate from the disorder helps her see that she is more than the disorder.

The opposite is also true. Sometimes people discount the disorder completely and believe that the individual just needs to "get over herself" or that she just wants attention. The dialectic is that the person with BPD has a disorder that is very difficult and that she must learn, with appropriate help, how to manage her emotions in a more effective way in order to lessen her suffering.

Dialectical Dilemmas for Family and Friends

As someone who cares about an individual with BPD, you are likely to experience some dialectical dilemmas in your relationship. Friends and family members, in my experience, find that they sometimes are over controlled with their responses to the person with BPD and at other times they are explosive. At times you do too much to help the person with BPD and at other times you do too little, less than you would do for any friend or family member, and pull way. At times you are overly confident in her ability to manage stress and cope effectively and at other times you have no confidence at all. Extremes create misery.

For each of the dialectic dilemmas below, write how you behave when you are at each pole of the dialectic. Then write what the synthesis would look like. The synthesis is when you take the most effective and the truth of each pole and move to a more effective response that is not an extreme.

Overcontrolled vs. Explosive

Overfunctioning vs. Pulling Away:

Overly worried vs. Over confident

Practice and Real World Application

Learning new ideas and skills takes time. Though you may be in a rush to learn what you can to help your relationship with your loved one, learning ideas without applying them will not be helpful. You'll have information that you know but not be able to use it to make a difference. I urge you to stop here. Practice dialectical thinking for a couple of weeks before moving on to other skills and ideas.

Every day, consider dialectics of your own thinking and that of others. When a friend talks about an experience she had, ask yourself what is missing from her description. When you find yourself disagreeing with someone's opinion, push yourself to find the truth in the other person's view. Then consider how your truth and the other person's truth could be put together in a meaningful way. When you have thoughts about a situation, particularly extreme thoughts, ask yourself to find the dialectic. Push yourself to use words implying connection instead of separation, such as using "and" instead of "but". Continue to practice after you have moved on to other skills until dialectical thinking becomes a habit.

4 SAVVY: SUPPORT, APPRECIATE, VALIDATE AND LOVE YOUR FRIEND OR FAMILY MEMBER WITH BPD

SAVVy is a guide to help you communicate more effectively with the person you love who has BPD. SAVVy stands for Support, Appreciate, Validate and LoVe Your Friend or Family Member with BPD. Supportive means for both you and your family member or friend diagnosed with BPD. Sometimes nothing you say or do gives you the results you want but we want to offer you the best tools we can to make an effective outcome more likely.

 Appreciate means that the positive, wonderful qualities of the person with BPD are remembered even when she is acting in ways that anger and frustrate you. Appreciate also means that we respect that what is right for one family may not be right for another. Appreciate means this communication program reflects that individuals with BPD are often delightful, fun, creative, passionate and caring people who can also behave in ways that are frustrating. Appreciate means that SAVVy recognizes that communication must include an understanding of the disorder and how the disorder affects interpersonal interactions. For example your loved one with BPD will benefit from spoken, direct reassurance that setting limits is not abandonment. Appreciate means knowing that individuals can manage the symptoms of the disorder and live a productive life. It also means recognizing that recovery is difficult but possible and that recovery does not mean being emotionally regulated one hundred per cent of the time. N one is always emotionally regulated, kind and thoughtful.

Validation is a key variable in how people are able to connect and form relationships. It's also a key variable in how people develop a sense of who they are—their identity. Validation is calming when people are upset and struggling to manage their emotions. And validation is a key component in communicating acceptance (Linehan, 1993). Everyone benefits from validation. Validating your own thoughts and feelings,accepting that you have needs and emotions, is important to help prevent burn-out and   to help you take care of yourself. Validation is one of the specific skills we'll address in detail in Chapters 10, 11, and 12.

Who hasn't regretted something they said in anger? Emotions overcome our logic and heated words that we could never imagine saying are flowing out of our mouths. Discussing issues or limits when emotionally overwhelmed is not effective. At the same time it's only human to be emotionally upset at times. We'll discuss what to do when you are too emotional to speak in respectful, loving ways or the individual with BPD is too upset to speak in respectful, loving ways.

Interpersonal Skills for Your Family means just that—we are offering skills for family members. The most important step you can take to help your loved one with BPD is to learn how to communicate effectively and how to interact in effective ways. Many families have reported that when they made changes, their loved one also made changes.

SAVVy

Support

For the individual with BPD

For family and friends

Appreciate

The positive qualities of the individual with BPD

The needs of the individual with BPD

How the illness affects interpersonal interactions

The needs of the family

What scientific research shows is effective

Different levels of recovery

Validate

The thoughts and emotions of the individual with BPD

The thoughts and emotions of other members of the family

Your own thoughts and feelings

V LoVe

Communicating and Behaving in Loving Ways, Regardless of the Emotion of the Moment

Y Your Friend or Family Member with BPD

Overview of SAVVy

Now we're ready to give you an overview of the specific skills that you will learn as part of SAVVy. The components of SAVVy are skills and information based on research and psychological principles. I haven't invented anything new but hope I've put the information together is a usable package that makes sense and is user friendly. I've listed all the skills in Chart B. You'll notice that the skills are divided into How and What Skills. This means we'll discuss what we have found to be effective and also how to do what is effective.

SAVVy: Supportive, Appreciative, Validating and Loving Interpersonal Skills for Your Family

HOW SKILLS

1: Set Your Intention and Know Your Goals for Your Interaction

Willingness and Acceptance

Willingness to Learn

Willingness to Accept the Diagnosis and Your Own Powerlessness

Understanding Myths that Make Acceptance Difficult

Willingness to Take Care of Yourself

2: Nourish Yourself

Reclaim/Create Your Identity

Focus Your Thoughts and Behaviors

Create Meaning

Find Support

Let Go of Shame and Guilt

Fill Yourself Up

3: BE CALMS

Calm voice, calm body language, maintain compassion

Accepting what you can't control

No Lectures/Defending/Attacking (yourself or others)

stay Mindful of Your Emotions

Separate--Mindfully Disengage

4: Practice

WHAT SKILLS

1: Listen with Wisdom

W Be Willing to check out what you think you are hearing

I Invest time in understanding their truth

S   Remember the Symptoms of BPD

D   Don't assume the person with BPD is okay

O   Only Tell the Truth

M Maintain Compassion and Respect

2: Double Check

3: Be Clear

    Personal limits

    Minding Your Own Chips

    Predictability

4: Validation

5: Understand Invalidation So You Don't Do It

6: My TALK Effective Communication Model

    My My point of view

    T   Tell the facts

    A   vAlidate, Assert your feelings, limits or ask a question

    L   Listen with WISDOM, vaLidate

    K   Keep to one point at a time

How Skills

When you understand the symptoms we discussed in the first chapter, you realize that most individuals with BPD, regardless of how they may seem on the outside, experience intense emotions that are painful and difficult to manage. They are more emotionally intense than someone who does not have BPD. They react more quickly and stay at a higher level of emotional arousal for a longer period of time (Linehan, 1993). Being emotional with someone who has BPD can be like throwing alcohol on a third degree burn. Your emotion adds to the emotion of the person with BPD, resulting in her having less ability to listen to you and to think wisely. Communication is usually ineffective when someone is emotionally distressed and it is especially so for someone with BPD. Staying calm is often not easy to do. The How Skills of staying calm includes taking care of yourself and committing to having a relationship with your loved one. Then in Step 3 you'll learn the How Skill of communicating in a calm way.

What Skills

Skill 1 is to **Listen with Wisdom**. One part of listening with wisdom is to check out the facts of body language. Body language is hard wired, so it's the same across cultures. Physical expression of anger is the same in China as it is in Chile, so we tend to believe nonverbal communication over verbal. Sometimes individuals with BPD have learned to hide their emotions well, many times because they've been told so many times they are overreacting or the way they feel is wrong. So the consumer you love can look in control on the outside and be in emotional turmoil on the inside. At the same time their body language may give you a clue that they are upset about something even their words say they are not.

Listening with Wisdom means to keep in mind the behaviors and urges and thoughts that influence the person with BPD. If you are talking about topics that you know could arouse distrust for someone who tends to be suspicious, then you might want to clarify those topics. If you are talking about statements that could bring up feelings of abandonment, then you may want to check to see if you are communicating your meaning clearly.

Skill 2 is to **Double Check**. Checking what you heard and what the consumer is hearing helps avoid the "what you heard is not what I said problem."

Skill 4 is to **Be Clear**. This means that you don't waffle about your position or what is expected. You state clearly what you are willing to do and what you are not willing to do.

Skill 5 is **Validation**. Validation is such an important part of communication with a consumer. We'll discuss the importance of validation, the prerequisites for practicing validation successfully and what obstacles you may encounter in practicing validation. We'll also give you opportunities to practice.

Real World Application

In this chapter we introduced the basic steps of SAVVy, our communication strategies for effective interpersonal relationships with consumers. Now that you understand the symptoms of BPD, and know the skills we'll be teaching. We're ready to get to the specifics and get started learning skills. In the next chapter we'll discuss the first step, Willingness and Acceptance.

The take home from this chapter is that if you want to communicate more effectively with an individual who has BPD or you want to support that person's recovery, the best steps you can take are to learn skills that help you manage your emotions more effectively and communicate in a different way. You may have focused on help as meaning that you assist the individual with BPD in making changes through giving them advice or pointing out their missteps. That would be easier than making changes yourself, and it doesn't work. The overview of SAVVy is to orient you to the changes in communication that you will be practicing. Accepting that the best way to help your loved one is through making changes yourself is a big step.

So for right now, the practice part is to stop telling your loved one what she or he should do differently. Watch yourself and count the number of times that you instruct, lecture, complain or criticize. Then stop.

5   SAVVY HOW SKILLS 1 AND 2

SAVVy How Skills are about the attitude and mindset you have when you learn and practice the What skills. Approaching the skills with an open mind and practicing them in a calm, gentle way enhances their effectiveness. If you practice the skills half-heartedly or with resentment, it is unlikely they will be effective.

How Skills 1: Set Your Intention and Know Your Goals

What is your intention right now with your loved one? Do you want to improve your relationship? Do you want to learn why she has this illness? Do you want to know what to do to protect yourself from pain? Or are you being pushed to do something you don't want to do? Do you believe she needs to change and you've already done enough or perhaps she is the one who has the problem so why should you do anything differently? Are you exhausted and just want her to get well quickly? Are you angry, feel trapped and resentful, and sometimes wish you never saw your loved one again?

Setting your intention is about you and what you want to accomplish. Being very honest about your intention, if only to yourself, is important. You will have difficulty achieving a goal that is not one you believe in or that you don't really want to achieve. If your intention is to learn ways to improve your relationship with your loved one or effective ways to communicate, then you are focusing on a specific intent, one that you can change. Keep this intention in your mind in every interaction and while you learn the skills in this book.

Remember the reason you are doing this. Knowing your goals is part of the way you will gauge your progress. Make your goals short-term and easily measured. Perhaps you want to have conversations about school or work without having them end in conflict. Whatever your goal, have a way that you measure it. Seeing your progress and achieving goals that match your intention will help you stay motivated. Write your goal down and track it for the next three to four months.

Setting Your Intention Worksheet

My primary reason for reading this book is:

I also have the following reasons:

So my intention is:

We can only change the things that are in our control. We can wish and hope and pray for events and situations and people to be different than they are, but when it comes down to what is possible for us, we can only change what is in our control.

How Skills 2: Willingness

Delaney is a sixty-two year old mother of Lisa, a thirty four year old woman with BPD. Delaney's usually very patient. One day she came to my office in tears. Lisa, in a rage because Delaney wouldn't give her money to pay for an apartment, broke a dish that belonged to Delaney's mother. Delaney lost her temper. She screamed at Lisa, calling her names and saying she couldn't take her behavior any more. Lisa yelled back, saying she knew her mother didn't love her anymore and she was sick of her mother always trying to control her. Then Lisa left the house. Delaney spent the rest of the night trying to find her, worried sick about her safety.

Families, friends, siblings, spouses, partners and others want to know how to help the individual with BPD and how to keep their loved one safe. I wish I knew a way we could end all suffering and stop all risky behaviors. When family members, spouses and friends regulate their emotions and solve their own problems in effective ways that is the most important step you can take to help the individual with BPD in her recovery.

Linehan (1993) describes the skill of Willingness for individuals with BPD. For family members willingness is an important first step toward improving your communication: willingness to learn new skills, to accept the disorder and your fears, to grieve, to take care of yourself, and to give up behaviors that aren't effective.

SAVVy HOW SKILLS: *Willingness*

Willingness to Learn New Skills

Willingness to Accept the Disorder

Willingness to Grieve and Accept Your Fears

Willingness to Take Care of Yourself

 A big part of willingness is accepting your own emotions. Emotions cannot be regulated if you try to ignore them. At the same time it is understandable that you may not want to feel such difficult feelings as fear of what might happen to someone we love. At times, we've all wished that life events were different. We may not have the life that we imagined when we were children or even in our early adulthood. Sometimes we can get stuck in how unfair a situation is. Our energy goes to imagining "what if" or to resenting what happened or maybe to feeling defeated and sad. Willingness means a readiness to go forward in the best way possible.

Willingness to Learn

Before you begin learning any new skills such as the ones we will describe here, it's critical that you believe in the importance and rightness of doing so and know that you are willing to do what it takes. Making changes of any kind is difficult. Learning how to validate someone with BPD and commit to practice the skill in your daily life will require time and effort on your part.

Perhaps most difficult of all, learning a new skill involves a period of frustration. You'll feel awkward and unnatural in the beginning and sometimes you'll forget to use the skill. You may judge yourself negatively because you aren't good at the skill and that naturally will create urges to quit. Learning new skills requires that you are willing to be a beginner. The way to be successful getting to your goal with so much work and frustration along the way is to be sure that the goal is necessary and worth it and to know that learning new skills will be frustrating. Learning new skills is difficult. Think how hard it is to change eating habits, even though you know that eating better nutrition has a big payoff for your energy level and your physical health. Success requires willingness and commitment: willingness to be in the world as it is, willing to participate imperfectly.

Willingness to Accept the Disorder

As a parent, most likely you have always wanted the best for your child. You've made sacrifices and done whatever you could to help throughout the years. Learning that your child has a disorder is painful. Realizing that there is no quick cure and that recovery from the disorder is long and often difficult is painful as well. Willingness does not mean that you welcome the news. Willingness means that you let go of your wishes and wants and are willing to participate by going forward with the best plan possible.

Acceptance means accepting reality as it is. You don't deny or pretend or let the information take over your life. You don't fight against what is true. It means you see life as it is. Acceptance is the opposite of denial. In Dialectical Behavior Therapy, Linehan emphasizes the importance of acceptance with a skill called Radical Acceptance.

When you are sailing and a storm comes up, what should you do? Most of us who aren't sailors would likely try to outrun the storm. But the best option is to sail into the storm. It won't be pleasant, there may be some really rough waves and maybe some seasickness, but you'll get through it faster than if than if you try to avoid it and it's safer. Accepting that the storm exists and that the best plan is to sail into the storm is difficult to do. Willingness is doing what you know is best. Can you picture the sailboat going as fast as it can and managing to stay in the storm as it moves along? If you sail into the storm instead, you will come out the other side and be through the storm faster. You can't outrun the storm. The storm is the painful situations that we experience in our lives.

In the book *Get Out of Your Mind and Into Your Head,* Steven Hayes (2005) gives the example of inviting all your relatives to your home for a party. You are excited and happy as favorite family members arrive. You're having great fun. Then the grumpy aunt you don't care for shows up. Slamming the door and not letting her in is one option. That would likely stop all the fun. The other guests would likely be affected and the grumpy aunt would become more and more the center of attention. You are unable to move, stuck holding the door.

When you are willful, you are like the person standing holding the door, trying to keep the unwanted aunt out.

Willingness is also allowing yourself to feel all the feelings that come with the diagnosis. Rumi wrote the following poem about accepting emotion.

The Guest House

This being human is a guest house.

Every morning a new arrival.

A joy, a depression, a meanness,

some momentary awareness comes

as an unexpected visitor.

Welcome and entertain them all!

Even if they're a crowd of sorrows,

who violently sweep your house

empty of its furniture,

still, treat each guest honorably.

He may be clearing you out

for some new delight.

The dark thought, the shame, the malice,

meet them at the door laughing,

and invite them in.

Be grateful for whoever comes,

because each has been sent

as a guide from beyond.

~ Rumi (1998) ~

Accepting that your child has any illness is difficult. Accepting that your child has Borderline Personality Disorder can be a challenge. The diagnosis used to mean that there was no known effective treatment and many therapists would refuse to see individuals with that diagnosis. Now there are therapists trained to treat people with BPD and recovery is possible. Still the treatment is lengthy and difficult. Sometimes patients can do well for a year or several years and then need to return to treatment. Treatment and recovery is often an ongoing process and a painful one for families and consumers alike. But it is treatable and people do recover.

Beliefs That Make Acceptance Difficult. There are several reactions to this diagnosis that make acceptance even more difficult. Many of these reactions involve self-blame or blaming of others. Blame is a particularly unhelpful reaction. It's like two people standing beside a car that ran out of gas and yelling at each other, "This is your fault. You were supposed to put gas in the car." Blaming doesn't get gas in the car or help prevent the problem from recurring.

It's my fault. Even if they have other children who do not have BPD, parents worry that they caused the disorder. In fact, for many years, an unhealthy parent—child relationship was considered a cause. Parents searching for reasons why their child has a disorder often feel guilty for losing their temper, not realizing their child was ill or not being a good parent for whatever reason. Yet many parents yell at their children, even neglect them, and their children do not have the disorder. We know now that there are likely multiple causes.

Some consumers have a history of traumatic events such as sexual or physical abuse, but many do not. And many people who have a history of sexual or physical abuse do not have BPD. We know there is a biological component to BPD and children with this biological predisposition may benefit from special parenting skills.

Most every parent wonders whether they have caused their child to develop Borderline Personality Disorder. There are different theories about the cause. Most all theories say it's a combination of environment and biology. For each person the percentage of environmental versus biological causes varies. For some BPD may be the result of primarily biological predisposition. For others it may be mainly an environmental. But according to the theory developed by Marsha Linehan, Ph.D., creator of Dialectical Behavior Therapy (DBT), the cause is transactional.

Transactional means that the environment and biology affect each other and change each other. For example, let's say one of your children is emotionally sensitive. Emotionally sensitive means they cry easily, cry longer, and cry more intensely than your other children. Perhaps all their emotions are more intense. You are at the theater with your three children and one of them kicks the sensitive one. The sensitive one starts crying and wants to tell you what his brother did. You tell him to be quiet, you'll talk about it later. That just makes him more upset and he cries louder. Then perhaps you tell him if he keeps on he will get a time out. He cries louder. You get more upset and tell him the kick couldn't have hurt that much and he is ruining the afternoon for the whole family over nothing. Maybe you add "like always." Your reaction to your son then escalates him more and his reaction upsets you more, none of which you wanted to happen..

See the problem? In the child's view, he was hurt by his brother and now you are angry with him. So he gets angrier. Your reaction seems completely unfair to him. In your view, your child is overreacting at a time that you most want him to calm down. It's a transaction with both people reacting to the other and building frustration in each other.

You have probably experienced two people reacting to each other until the conflict is more about reacting to each other than the original issue. Many parents are embarrassed by their behavior, how they have lost their tempers and said hurtful statements to their children who have BPD. They felt horribly guilty afterwards, but they became so emotionally flooded that they spoke out of anger and frustration.

Perhaps you have never lashed out at anyone like you do with your child with BPD. That may lead you to blame the child for your behavior. Perhaps you alternate between blaming yourself and blaming your child. As she grows older, your child is likely to do the same. At times she will see you as a punitive, uncaring parent who doesn't understand her and at other times will be horrified at the way she has treated you, her loving and supportive parent.

The truth is neither of you is to blame. Your child has a disorder that unfortunately leads her to behave in confusing ways that can be frustrating to those who love her. Parenting or having a relationship with someone who has BPD will require learning skills to manage your emotions. The child is not wrong for being sensitive but must learn ways to manage her feelings.

He could do better if he just would. . .Sometimes it's hard to believe that someone who is so talented, outgoing, bright and entertaining could have a disorder. If he can be so caring and thoughtful sometimes then that means he can do it all the time. The main issue with BPD is an inability to manage emotions. So when they are content or upbeat, you see them at their best. When their emotions change to anger or sadness, they cannot manage the emotions and their behavior changes. In addition, individuals with BPD have developed skills at hiding the turmoil they feel inside. So sometimes they look and act competent when they are feeling miserable. They can only keep the façade up so long.

I'm a failure as a parent. Because your child has an illness does not mean you failed as a parent. There are parents who were completely ineffective in parenting and their children do not have BPD. There are parents who are experts in parenting and practice the best skills and their children are diagnosed with BPD. In any given family, one child may have BPD and another doesn't. Having a child diagnosed with BPD may mean you need to learn new ways to parent, to become a specialized parent, but it doesn't mean you are at fault. Blame isn't helpful.

S/he will never_____. Sometimes you've had dreams for your children that are difficult to give up. Maybe the dreams are the same dreams many parents have, such as her having a family and sharing the life of your grandchildren in a peaceful way. Or maybe you fear she will never find contentment because she has this disorder. Maybe you're in despair, feeling trapped in a situation that you cannot manage and do not see a way for it to be different. What you imagined your relationship to be may not be possible. Accepting that is difficult but opens the door to consider the options that are possible. Research shows that therapy can make a difference. Recovery is hard work that only the consumer can do, but recovery is possible.

I have to find a solution. I have to fix this for my child. Regardless of the cause of the problems, your child has to work to overcome them. It would be nice if there were a pill or some medical procedure that could cure BPD. It would be wonderful if parents could cure BPD. The only way for the consumer to get relief from BPD is through the hard work of therapy. And they have to be willing to do that work. Families have different reactions to learning their loved one has BPD. Some parents/spouses are relieved to get the diagnosis. The diagnosis finally explains what their child or spouse has been going through. Understanding the diagnosis gives them hope for recovery and shows them the steps to take to make a difference. Knowing what you can do and finding the most effective treatment is empowering.

Whatever your reaction, the important point is to not judge yourself for it. Your reaction, given what you have experienced, fits what you feel and think. Accepting your own emotions and thoughts will help you work through your grief and find your own peace.

When you are given the diagnosis and told there is no medication, no hospital that can cure BPD, well, that's a hard fact to accept about someone you love. You may be angry at the doctors, angry at God, angry at yourself, angry at your child and angry at the world. You may be sad, scared, and/or hopeless. You may feel despair.

Resisting what we cannot change creates and prolongs suffering, like trying to outrun the storm in your sailboat instead of sailing into it and learning how to manage the boat in storm conditions. So the first step is to accept that you cannot fix this disorder for your loved one. Acceptance does not mean giving up. Acceptance does not mean you lose hope. On the contrary acceptance allows you to move forward, get support and get the best possible information about what is in your control. You can learn effective skills that can help. So grieving is normal. Let yourself grieve.

Maybe you have myths that you believe about BPD. Let's take a look at what you are telling yourself about BPD. Read each of the myths below and then write the reason the myth is not true.

Myths That Make Acceptance Difficult

Worksheet

My loved one's illness is my fault.

Dispute:

I have to fix this for my child.

Dispute:

I cannot live my own life until s/he is well.

Dispute:

I have to plan my schedule around my loved one's needs.

Dispute:

I can't think about my own needs because I have to take care of my loved one's needs.

Dispute:

I am a failure because my loved one has borderline personality disorder.

Dispute:

S/he needs me to manage her emotions.

Dispute:

If I accept the illness then I'll have no hope .

Dispute:

If she has BPD or other emotion dysregulation disorder, she can never be happy.

Dispute:

Willingness to Grieve

Every parent wants the best for their children. Learning that your child has Borderline Personality Disorder can be heart breaking. Some of the information on the Internet can be discouraging and by the time you have the diagnosis you have likely experienced many painful experiences. Accepting that your child has a disorder brings the pain of grieving.

When you learn your child has a disorder. Sometimes you will have to put on hold or give up some of the dreams you had for your child. At times the disorder may be so severe that you worry about her future. Perhaps your child has been unusually successful to a point, then been unable to manage their life. That is what happened with Dixie. Dixie's parents were very proud of her achievements. Dixie graduated from a top-rated law school and landed a job at a New York firm. She worked her way up to junior partner before she made a suicide attempt, then took a leave of absence for a year. Ten years later she has not been able to return to work. She is employed part-time in a clothing store and struggles to manage her daily life. Her parents grieve that she is not able to be self-supporting and to make use of her law degree and that she suffers periods of depression. At the same time they love her and accept that the stress of legal work is not helpful for her.

As a family member you may be confused, and angry that your loved one struggles with BPD. Perhaps you have sought help from numerous health care providers with no results, no answers. You would do almost anything to help your child and yet you feel so helpless. Knowing your child is suffering intense pain and the treatment takes time is painful.

Denial, anger, fear, despair are all part of the grief process. When you love someone with BPD the grieving process may be recurrent. New issues arise that cause difficulties and your loved one may have multiple ups and downs on the path to recovery.

What do I mean by not holding on to the grieving? You hold on to emotions by ruminating about situations that bring about the emotion, by thinking over and over about the situation. Letting go of the grieving means feeling the emotion but not making it stronger by ruminating. Taking the guilt, hurt, anger, and fear and channeling it into effective action can help lessen the pain you feel.

Willingness to Take Care of Yourself

Burnout is defined as exhaustion of physical or emotional strength or motivation usually as a result of prolonged stress or frustration. Emotional burnout is more likely if you do not take care of yourself, do not set limits, and block your emotions. When you are in burn out you are so tired and drained you feel you can't do anymore. Sometimes you wonder if you still care.

Effectively dealing with long-term stress without getting burned out requires getting support and finding ways to cope with stress. Effective coping would also mean confronting your own denial, false hopes or feelings of helplessness. Fighting your emotions is tiring. It takes energy to not recognize feelings. So being willing to feel your emotions helps you decrease your own emotional reactivity and increases the likelihood you will be able to validate when you are in an emotional interaction with your loved one. Feeling helpless often leads to depression and lack of action. And while you are helpless to wipe out the illness or to change your loved one, you are not helpless in other ways. Building a sense of mastery in the situation by acquiring knowledge and understanding your options is healing.

When you are in burn out, you need a break, if at all possible. If you can, find a way to take a vacation. If you can get regular breaks that can be very helpful. Though it may seem impossible, keep pleasurable activities in your life and maintain relationships with friends. Be careful of letting your loved one's disorder take over your life. Recovery from BPD is not a sprint but a marathon, for both the individual diagnosed with BPD and those who care about her.

Take care of your health. Too little sleep, not enough food, not taking needed medication, drinking too much and the amount of cumulative stress you've experienced all add to your burnout.

Real World Application

In this chapter we discussed effective ways family members could begin their work to help their loved one diagnosed with BPD. Specific situations that require skills include dealing with accepting the reality of the diagnosis, grieving without getting stuck, and coping effectively so as to not get burned out.

By far most families do the best that they can with the knowledge and resources they have and they make mistakes. Biology plays a part in who develops BPD and it is impossible to determine specifically how much of the cause is inherited and how much is environmental. Blaming yourself or your loved one or anyone else just isn't helpful. Blame is not part of a solution and only wastes time and energy and damages relationships. When you find yourself thinking in blaming terms, notice and label those as unhelpful thoughts. Then gently move on. Distract your mind if you need to. Practicing thinking in a different way can create new patterns of thinking.

6 LETTING GO OF WHAT DOESN'T WORK

George's teenage daughter was diagnosed with BPD. She repeatedly had car accidents because she would drive when she was angry and not pay attention to the road. The last time she wrecked her car George told her this was the last time he was buying her a new one. When she wrecked it, George said no, that was it, he was done. He stood firm through her crying and pleading. Then she stopped talking to him, except to say that her life wasn't worth living because she couldn't see her friends anymore. Fearing the worse, he gave in.

Nobody wants to spend time, energy, and effort to support and help a loved one in a way that it doesn't work. It's discouraging for everyone. The helper feels ineffective. The person being helped is likely to feel hopeless. Why would anyone act in ways that don't work? Actually, there are several good reasons that parents and spouses and friends continue to help in ways that don't work.

Difficulty in Maintaining Your Limits

Finding a way to cope with the difficulties suffered by people with BPD is not easy. For most, it is a process, with many ups and downs. There is no one way to cope, no just do this and it will be okay. But we do know some behaviors and choices that often make the situation worse and some behaviors and choices that can help both you and the consumer. You may know what is too much for you and what is not and still do more than you are comfortable doing for your loved one.

You don't want to upset your loved one more than she already is. Doing what she wants, regardless of whether it helps her in the long run, makes you feel better. You worry about her. Surely you can help her out until she gets better.

Then everything will be different. The truth is that recovery from BPD is a long process and it's not a stage or a "rough period" that will pass. Recovery from BPD is gradual and requires that the person with BPD do things differently.

You are burned out. You love your daughter/spouse but you've helped so much, worried so much, you can't do anymore. You are so upset that you find little joy in your life. How can you smile when she is so depressed? So you avoid, ignore, or just do what is easiest because you don't have the energy to act in more effective ways.

You can't do what you don't know. You've made the best choices you could but sometimes what feels right isn't what works.

You are afraid of your loved one's emotions. You'd do anything to avoid her being angry with you or in becoming more depressed because the consequences of either of those are terrifying.

The problem is that not addressing problems and your own needs may actually make the problems worse in the long run. When you don't address issues, your not doing so says that you think your loved one isn't capable of hearing the feedback or of understanding your feelings and rights. Whether you mean to or not your behavior communicates that you don't think she can function like other adults in the same situation. Now you may be saying, "That's because she can't."

There is a dialectic here. Remember that dialectic means possibility of two opposite ideas both being true. In this case, let's say it's true that the consumer has not ever listened to feedback from you without getting upset. The dialectic, or the opposite, is that she must learn to accept feedback without getting upset in order to function as an adult. Your loved one may not have the skills to accept reasonable feedback and/or be empathic about your viewpoint. That may be true. But how will she learn to accept feedback and be empathic if she isn't given opportunities to learn? And no, there isn't a limit on those opportunities. You don't say, "I've done it a hundred million times and that's enough. No more chances."

When you say that, unfortunately that means you're giving up or giving in. That's an expected reaction after a period of time with no change in behavior. For your loved one, not being empathic with you is likely part of the way she gets her needs met. There will have to be a reason for that behavior to change. That reason may well need to be that you are saying no and not meeting her needs when she is behaving in ways that are harmful to you.

That's fine, you might say, for the consumer who is seeking help and actively working on recovery. But what about the loved one who refuses therapy and has no one helping her to understand that accepting feedback and treating others in a certain way is part of her developing a more enjoyable life? What good does it do to go through the same hurtful pattern over an over, such as giving feedback that you need to give but that only results in her being upset?

Having the same hurtful interaction in the same way is unlikely to lead to any positive changes. This is one of the reasons that learning skills for yourself is one of the most helpful actions you can take for your loved ones recovery. You cannot control your loved one but you can control your own behavior.

You see, interpersonal interactions are transactional, not one way. This means if you and I are having a conversation, then what you say affects me and what I say affects you and the conversation goes a certain way because of our reactions to each other. If you started the same conversation with a different person it would proceed differently because the other person's reactions would be different. You would respond to his reactions, thus changing the conversation from your previous one.

Here's an example. Jill puts on her favorite pair of blue jeans. Her husband says, "I like how those jeans are tight on you." Jill says, "You think I'm fat. So what if I've gained a few pounds, so have you and you don't hear me saying anything." Her husband responds, "I'm not 18 anymore. I know I've gained some weight, but do you always have to criticize me and jump on everything I say?" Jill responds, "You started it." Her husband walks out, slamming the door. See how Jill reacted to her husband's comments and he in turn reacted to hers? This is how arguments start over nothing. This interaction could have gone this way. Jill puts on her favorite pair of jeans. Her husband says, "I like how those jeans are snug on you." She says, "Yeah? Thanks." He smiles and kisses her goodbye.

So if you learn skills to manage your own reactions and feelings, the interaction with your loved one has to be different because you will affect her differently.

Let Go of Avoiding

Many times parents and spouses don't want to upset the person who has BPD, so they keep information from them. The problem is that then the individual with BPD doesn't trust you. She wonders what you are keeping from her and may imagine that you are keeping information that you are not.

In addition, the individual with BPD doesn't get to practice managing such situations. Sometimes parents/spouses wait for a time when they think the person can accept the news better, like when they are coping more effectively. Sometimes they don't want to tell them upsetting news when they are doing well because it could cause them to backslide. Sometimes it seems there is no good time to give difficult information, so parents and spouses avoid doing it as long as possible. Their intention is good and it makes sense that family members wouldn't want to cause upset to someone who is emotionally reactive.

Unfortunately, while it may sound reasonable, this is a form of family members attempting to manage the consumer's emotions. However, the information usually comes out and then you are blamed for keeping information from them. The paranoia/suspiciousness that is often present with BPD may be activated and they will wonder what else you are keeping from them, to the point of questioning most everything you say and do. Like many of BPD symptoms, that reaction is understandable, but goes to the extreme.

Consider this example. Nicole is a stay at home mother of two boys and a girl. Her youngest, Alicia, is 18, in her senior year of high school and still lives at home. Nicole sees her daughter as choosing her boyfriend over her. She is angry that her daughter doesn't share all her thoughts, experiences, and feelings with her. She rages at her husband and her daughter on a regular basis. Nicole's husband attempts to protect Alicia from her mother's anger, even saying "Let's not tell your Mom about this. It will just upset her." He makes many of the parenting decisions without telling Nicole. He avoids telling Nicole about problems in his business and when he has to give her upsetting information he waits for the best possible time.

As a result Nicole is furious that he is keeping information from her and constantly wonders what he is not telling her. When he does give her information that she knows he has been withholding, her anger is out of control. The avoidance only makes the situation worse.

Let Go of Pleading/Reasoning with Emotions.

Many parents/spouses attempt to reason or use logic with the consumer in their life.. They will make statements like the following: "Honey, we simply can't afford to pay for any more classes if you are just going to drop out again." "We can't afford to pay any more of your credit card bills. You'll just have to pay them yourself next time. We need some savings for retirement." "This constant rollercoaster isn't good for your mother's health. We can't do it anymore." "I'm going to lose my job if I take any more time off work. You'll have to manage until I come home."

All the above make perfect sense. But emotions don't respond to logic and individual with BPD is reacting to emotion. So when you try to use logic in response to her emotion or to try to calm her emotion, that will not work. Whenever the consumer is in an emotional state, then use validation. Later, when the consumer is calmer, she is more likely to hear logic. Use validation and then present facts when your loved one is calmer and can listen.

Let Go of Expressing Out of Control Emotions

Yelling at someone with borderline personality disorder doesn't help her change her behavior. Neither does blaming them or accusing them or shaming them. Sometimes it feels as if using power or making someone feel ashamed of what they have done would help them change their behavior, but that is not the case. These techniques are not effective in helping anyone change their behavior and are particularly not helpful to individuals with BPD. Your losing control does not model effective behavior for them.

People with BPD may act impulsively in the moment and have difficulty thinking ahead. When they are acting on their emotions they are not thinking that later you will be angry or hurt. Often cause and effect relationships aren't clear to them at all.

In addition, at the time you are yelling, the person with BPD may be overwhelmed by the emotion you're creating and unable to listen. Perhaps because of the emotional overload they dissociate and are not even present with you. If they dissociate then they will not remember what you said to them and it will make no difference in their behavior.

Let Go of Helping Too Much

Individuals with BPD often have difficulty with adult responsibilities and tasks. Spouses and parents may understandably see them as child-like in those ways. But to treat them as if they are children is not helpful to either party. Taking care of rent, tax issues, medical appointments, complaints to service providers, all that may be easier for you to do than for your daughter. However, you only want to give as much help as she needs. For example, if she isn't able to manage paying her bills, then maybe do it with her or give her less money more frequently. You might devise a system of managing money, such as using envelopes labeled with the amount needed for each bill, that works for the consumer. If you aren't sure how much help your loved one needs, consider a meeting with her and her therapist.

I wish there were a magic pill that could ease the suffering of all those who suffer from BPD. I also wish there was a magic therapy that could cure BPD in a few months or a way that parents could cure their children. I wish there was a way that parents and spouses could get their loved ones to work in treatment when they don't want to go to treatment. I wish all that and more. Unfortunately there is no magic pill at this point and there is no quick fix and there is no way parents and spouses can make someone want to work in therapy.

Many people who suffer with BPD hope for rescue and understandably so. Going to treatment is painful, talking about feelings is painful, going over experiences that have made you feel ashamed and crazy is painful. Many individuals with BPD have been to treatment and it hasn't worked. That is discouraging.

When someone you love is suffering so much, you naturally want to find a solution. If that would work, I'd be all for it. Unfortunately it doesn't work. You can't make their feelings less intense or painful. You can't force them to be committed to therapy.

Give Up Rigid Rules That Don't Work

One approach that is sometimes recommended to parents is to refuse to have a relationship with the consumer or refuse to give any support unless they change their behavior. Basically the approach means that you don't give your adult daughter financial assistance unless she gets a job. You don't give her extra help or money and you don't help keep her out of jail or avoid any other consequences of her behavior. You don't bend and you allow her to feel the full consequences of her behavior.

In my opinion, this approach is not helpful for someone with BPD and may in fact aggravate the symptoms. If they feel abandoned by their family that will only create more emotional turmoil which makes it more difficult for them to think wisely.

The approach that is most likely to work is more flexible. Keeping your relationship if at all possible is important. You continue to love the individual with BPD though you may not be willing to provide extra money to pay a ticket. You may decide to stick to a certain monthly allowance and not allow her to move home but take her food and gifts at times. What works for you may not work for someone else.

The answer as to how much help to give isn't black and white and it isn't one that can be easily answered. Basically, the answer is to never do for your child what she can do for herself. If the task is something she can't do for herself, then you need to assist her with only the part she cannot do. If you do something for her that she can do for herself, you limit her growth. If you push her to do something that she cannot do, you may create feelings of shame or being overwhelmed, perhaps feelings of rejection. The tightrope is a difficult one to walk.

Let Go of Reinforcing Behaviors You Don't Want and Punishing Behaviors You Do Want

There are certain ways that we learn the ways we behave whether we are aware of what is happening or not.

Coco is a very hungry one hundred pound Golden Retriever. He would eat all day long if I let him. To manage his weight, I started giving him frozen fruit and veggies in a kong, a rubber container with a small opening so that he has to work to get the food out. He loves his kongs. I've been doing a lot of work at home lately. Coco would go and stand at the refrigerator, obviously letting me know he wants a kong. I would only give him three a day and I didn't like being interrupted from my writing so I would ignore him. When I got up to do something else, such as let him go out the door to the yard, I would sometimes give him a kong while I was up.

Coco learned to control me. He would go to the door and make a whine like he had to go outside. Then when I got up, walked to the door to let him out, he would back up and go to the refrigerator, only a few steps away. Coco was modifying my behavior. He knew the behavior he wanted to increase (my giving him kongs) and he found a way that worked, at least until I caught on.

Reinforcement

The consequences that follow a behavior will either increase or decrease the behavior. If you are complimented when you wear a certain color, you will be more likely to buy clothes in that color when you have the opportunity. If you receive more money for selling chocolates than for selling pencils, you are more likely to sell chocolates. If someone stops yelling at you when you do what they want (relief), you are likely to do what they want whenever possible. This is called positive reinforcement. Positive reinforcers are the consequences that increase the likelihood of a behavior occurring. When you reward yourself with a new dress because you lost five pounds, you have given yourself a positive reinforcer. When you get relief from something you don't like, such as someone crying or yelling or driving too fast, then that is a negative reinforce.

Punishment

Eric lives with his family in a small town near a large city. Eric is 21, doesn't have a job, and he spends most of his day playing video games. Whenever his mother says something to him about helping around the house or getting a job, Eric talks about how miserable he is and how no one will hire him and what a loser he is, good for nothing and just a burden to his parents. His anguish is so upsetting that his mother has stopped bringing up any suggestions that Eric do any chores. In this case a behavior if followed by a response or consequence that makes the behavior less likely to occur. That's punishment. Eric punished his mother for asking him to do chores or get a job, though he may not have been aware of the effect of his behavior.

Extinction

Extinction means that you stop reinforcing a behavior. If you realize that the more you pay attention to your son when he skips classes, the more frequently he skips, then you may decide that your attention is a reinforcer for him, even though you are giving him negative attention. If your attention is a reinforcer that is maintaining the behavior, then not paying attention to the behavior would stop the behavior from occurring. You withdraw the reinforcer (your attention).

When you stop reinforcing a behavior that was previously reinforced, the behavior tends to increase for a short period of time. This is caused a behavioral burst and is only temporary. So your son might skip class even more frequently when you stop paying attention to his behavior. This increase is only temporary. If you continue to ignore the behavior, completely ignore the behavior, no facial expressions or exacerbation sounds, it will stop.

Shaping

You may have seen animals do amazing tricks, like a pigeon play a small piano or a dog bark out a song. When trainers work with animals they teach one small step at a time. That's called shaping. When you are attempting to change your behavior you might use the same techniques. You might reward yourself for walking through the gym, then for staying for five minutes, then for getting on the treadmill, etc. Shaping is usually used when the behavior you are attempting to teach or learn is difficult.

You probably know some ineffective behaviors that you exhibit with your loved one. Perhaps you avoid discussing important topics for fear of your loved one's reaction or you become overwhelmed with sadness to the point you have difficulty functioning when your loved one is not doing well. So the first step is in using behavioral principles to change your behaviors that aren't effective.

Let Go of What Doesn't Work

Our own behaviors are subject to punishment and reinforcement. When you want to change behavior, considering what is reinforcing or punishing your behavior and changing those consequences will help you make the changes you want to make.

To better understand how your responses might be influencing your loved one's behavior, keep track for a week. First identify a behavior. Be very specific, such as she complains of being sick whenever you ask her to go to the store. For a week, record what your response is. What do you do when she complains of being sick? Don't change your response just record it. Then record what she does in response to whatever it is that you do.

Behavior   **My Response**   **Her Response to My Response**

1

2

3

4

5

If she continues to do the same behavior over and over, and so do you, then change your response. Try extinguishing her response, or reinforcing a different response, or using negative reinforcement. For example you don't stop talking for three minutes every day about the issue until she does what you have asked her to do. You don't yell, you just calmly keep talking about needing something from the store and how nice it would be if she got it for you. Pay attention to her behavior. What does she do? Fill out the form again with the your new response and record how she responds. Remember you will not likely get perfection and eagerness but you will get a behavior change.

Changing Expectations

If you have set up expectations that aren't helpful, such as your child expects you to give her extra money whenever she asks for it, changing that expectation will be difficult. Most likely you have told her many times that she must stick to her budget and that you aren't going to give her extra money any more, that this time is the last time. Then you do again.

To change this pattern you will need to interact differently from the very beginning. If you have never given her a written agreement, then do that. Sit down with her when she doesn't need money, perhaps when you are giving her the weekly amount you provide her, and have a conversation. Remember to validate her and her needs as well as your own needs.

"I know that managing money is not your strong point and that you have unexpected expenses that make budgeting difficult. I love you and I want to help you, and I know that by giving you extra money I am not helping you learn to budget and it is frustrating to me. In addition, I can't afford to continue to give you so much extra every month. I've made a list of the items

I will pay for and of the spending money I will give you each week. Please look it over and see if there is anything I have missed and let me know. I think this plan will help make it easier for both of us and help us not argue over money. I know I haven't kept our agreements in the past, but please know that for both of our sakes I will keep this one and I hope you do too."

Even when you give difficult information in the best way possible, the person receiving the information will likely be upset. Using validation will help but in particularly difficult conversations will not erase the dysregulation. Keep validating as that will help the other person get back in control of her emotions.

Worksheet on Changing Patterns

The following worksheet may help you keep your commitment to change behaviors that aren't effective. General behaviors you might want to consider, such as avoiding and being controlled by your loved one's emotions are listed below. Choose a specific behavior that fits in the category and then choose one step to change the behavior. For example, if you avoid balancing your checkbook because you don't want to know how much money you've given to the person you love, then the first step might be to look at the funds remaining in your account on a consistent basis without adding up the amounts. Then the next step might be to add the amounts so you know the total.

Worksheet   Patterns of Behavior You Want to Change

Specific Behavior :

First or Next Step to Changing This Pattern:

Goal Date:

Date Achieved:

Repeat the process until you have changed the behavior you want to change.

Categories of Behaviors

Being Controlled by Emotions

Avoiding

Managing Others' Emotions

Pleading/Reasoning with Emotion

Losing Control of Your Anger

Rescuing

Being Rigid

So now you've made your commitments and set your first step that you want to take. Notice that we've asked you to list what behavior you will use instead of the old behavior. It's important to have a new behavior to replace what you were doing before or to help you get closer to the goal you want to achieve. The next chapters will offer you new ways of communicating.

Real World Application

In this chapter we covered behaviors of family members that tend to occur in reaction to BPD symptoms but do not facilitate the recovery of the person diagnosed or the well-being of the family. It's natural to do what you think will help and what has helped in other situations. You want to help the person you love. Individuals with BPD have different ways of reacting than other people and more sensitive emotions. The most effective ways to communicate and interact are not the same. The best choice for supporting them in their recovery is to learn skills of communication for yourself that are more effective.

This chapter is about changing the focus from your loved one to yourself. What can you do differently in problem interactions? If there is a recurring issue that is painful for both of you, look at your own behavior. You may be doing nothing wrong. You probably aren't. Asking your loved one to stick to a budget isn't wrong. This is not about right and wrong. It's about what works. If what you are doing isn't working, even though you think it should work, then try something different. For example, if you give your loved one money for rent but the rent doesn't get paid, consider other ways such as paying the landlord directly. Accept that doing the same behavior over and over is likely to have the same result.

7 HOW SKILLS 3: NOURISH YOURSELF

When you become a parent, your child consumes your life. Your identity becomes mostly about being a mother or a father. The majority of your day and what you do is about your child. Yet, the process of parenting is one of separation. As the child grows and matures he becomes more and more independent until your identity no longer must be wholly based on your being a parent. Many parents are challenged to redefine their identity when they no longer need to devote themselves to their children. The process is difficult. How can it be that the cute little two year old is now twenty-five? If your son or daughter has struggled with mental health issues, the separation may be even more difficult. Parents want to solve problems for their child. Perhaps they are scared what will happen if they don't.

Not solving problems for your adult son or daughter may be terrifying. Over years of crises you may be on constant alert, waiting for the next episode. You may have urges to call many times a day and constantly think about what she might be doing. Your mind may be constantly thinking about what might upset her and how upsets could be avoided. You may have situations that you constantly replay in your head, perhaps even nightmares. Whatever family events are planned your thoughts may be about how our son or daughter will handle them. Perhaps you are incapacitated to the point of staying in bed when your loved one is depressed.

When you have an adult child with BPD, you may be driven to spend your days waiting for phone calls or wondering how s/he is doing. You may feel and believe that you must be available for your son or daughter. Perhaps you are exhausted from being on alert, waiting for the next crisis. You find that you are too absorbed with your loved one's life that you don't have time or energy for your own. The same may be true for a spouse or a sibling or a friend of someone with BPD. This feeling is common and compelling.

Getting out of this cycle may seem impossible.

Even as you read this you may be saying to yourself that you have no time to have your own life as you must be available if your loved one needs you. Any other focus or activity may seem meaningless and hold little interest to you.

Giving up the idea that you can manage your loved one's emotions and behaviors may leave a feeling of emptiness and fear. So much of your life and energy has been about your loved one, how could there not be a difficult transition? Probably the last thing you want to do is figure out your own identity separate from your son or daughter or spouse. Who has time for that? Nothing could be as important as someone you love needing you.

Reclaim Your Identity

Having your own life and identity is one of the how steps for families. Having your life revolve around an adult child with BPD sends the message to her that you believe she cannot manage without you In addition, it fosters the illusion that you are responsible for your loved one's emotions and behaviors or that you can control her emotions and behaviors. So having your own life and your own identity separate from your loved one is a key step in our program.

When you were younger, what was your passion? What did you want to do? Did you have a desire to travel? To paint? To work with the elderly? To sail? To teach? To learn a different language? Dance? Be more active in your church? Consider what your interests used to be as that may be a good place to start to find activities that you can do now. What about friends that you may have stopped seeing over the years? Maybe get in touch with them again. If you've kept your interests and friends then begin to spend more time involved with them. Be patient as you will be getting to know your own interests and develop friendships and that may take time. Plus it is likely that nothing will seem interesting in the beginning because you will be experiencing withdrawal from crisis addiction.

If you've kept your interests and friends then begin to spend more time involved with them. Put effort into strong relationships with other family members, friends and colleagues.

The change of moving more into your own life and identity doesn't need to be an all or none action. Gradually spending more time with friends and gradually doing more activities that you enjoy is likely to be the best strategy.

Focus Your Thoughts

Whenever you notice that you are thinking about your loved one in a worried way and there is no immediate reason for this, change your thoughts. Say "stop" gently to yourself. Then you may want to think how much you love her and send loving thoughts her way. Maybe you want to send thoughts of wishing her well, particularly if you are angry with her. Changing your thoughts from "How could she do that" to "I wish her well" helps you to move forward. When you wish her well or send her loving thoughts, it only works if your intention is true, that you truly do wish her well.

Remind yourself that you cannot control his or her decisions. Then push your mind to think of something different. Don't let yourself drive by every day just to check on her or spend your shopping trip looking for something you think he would like to have. Sometimes physical exertion helps to focus thoughts, so exercise may help. Though you may have the urge to isolate, being with other people helps keep your mind off your loved one. Progress is likely to be slow. You will probably find yourself having to change your thoughts many times an hour in the beginning. But persistence will work.

Keep your family relationships about more than your loved one's disorder. Commit to having conversations in which you don't discuss her well-being. Engage in activities that aren't about the disorder. Spend time with friends when you talk about other aspects of your life. Work to assure that your family does not revolve around the disorder.

At the same time, give yourself set times that you can focus on your worries and concerns. Give yourself fifteen minutes to just think about your concerns. Schedule a time to worry. Then whenever worries come into your head, tell yourself you'll think about that at the assigned time.

Create Meaning

Engaging in activities and causes that you find meaningful is another way to help you reclaim or change your identity. Providing a service to others or making a difference politically could help you feel positive about the change you can make happen, the change that is in your control. Maybe you will volunteer with the elderly or children. Maybe you will be a tutor or volunteer in an animal shelter. For some meaning comes through spirituality or faith.

Find Support

What is supportive is different from one person to another. Joining a support group, where others understand the challenges involved in loving someone with BPD, a place to check out your thinking, may be right for you. Other places to get support include friends, church, and family. Perhaps you need more than these options could offer. Then you could see a therapist who is knowledgeable about BPD.

Let Go of Shame and Guilt

One of the biggest reasons family members don't reach out for support and help is because they feel guilty and ashamed. Guilty about their parenting and ashamed that someone in their family has a serious mental disorder. They may try to hide it or keep it in the family. They may be willing to get help for the consumer but not for themselves. In fact, shame and guilt may be one of the biggest roadblocks to families getting into recovery. In Chapter 16, Jim and Diane Hall discuss their own experience with shame and guilt and how they overcame it.

Shame and guilt are different. Brene Brown (2010) says that shame is about who you are and guilt is about what you did. You feel guilty that you yelled at your daughter and you feel shame that you are a bad mother. Justified guilt serves the purpose of helping us stick to our moral values; from behaving in inappropriate ways that hurt other people. Justified shame helps us keep our behavior acceptable to the groups we value and need to belong to for our own survival. When shame and guilt are justified, you make amends in some way, repair or make up for what you have done, work to change your behavior and accept the consequence gracefully. By facing the situation and the people involved, you learn from your transgressions and don't repeat the same hurtful behavior patterns. The problem is when these emotions are unjustified—the person is feeling guilt when they are not responsible or feeling shame when there is no threat of expulsion from the group that is important to them (Linehan, 2011). Families of consumers we've worked with often feel guilty, believing that they have done something to cause the illness. They also feel shame as if the consumer's illness is a judgment of them as parents and people.

When people feel shame they tend to hide and isolate which limits the support they can get from others. It also tends to lead to their seeing themselves as able to live their lives again only when the consumer is well. When shame and guilt are unjustified, it is important to not isolate or hide. Be open with others about your feelings and why you feel the way you do. Accepting the feelings and letting go of your judgment of yourself is part of moving past shame and guilt. Moving past is to focus on your current behavior, be mindful of the present, and when your mind wanders to the past gently bring it back to the present with acceptance.

Worksheet: Shame and Guilt

For each sentence, write as many reasons you feel shame and guilt as you can think of. Spend some time with this. Do an inventory of your relationship with the individual who has BPD. After you are finished, then go back and identify whether the guilt and shame are just justified or not. This is a skill from DBT that was developed by Marsha Linehan (1993).

Shame and Guilt Feelings	**Useful or Not Useful**

I feel shame about…

I feel guilty about…

Now, consider what action you will take. For useful guilt (you really did something wrong) you may want to make amends in some way.

Action Plan for Useful Guilt

(Repair, Amends, Commit to different behavior, accept consequences, live in the present not the past)

Action Plan for Guilt That is Not Useful

(Ways to keep doing what you are doing and let your thoughts just pass)

Action Plan for Shame That is Not Useful

(Ways to hold your head up and face the truth)

Fill Yourself Up. Create feelings other than distress and worry about your loved one. While those feelings will be there, with practice and effort other feelings can co-exist with the worry. Feeling content with nature or laughing at a funny movie could be helpful. Engage in activities that absorb your thinking and feel nurturing, Get massages, have your nails done, read a good book, cook your favorite foods, listen to soothing music—whatever helps rejuvenate you, do it! Actively create good experiences to have good memories in order to build up your emotional reserves.

Worksheet: Nourish Yourself

Use this workshop to keep track of the ways that you increase what you do to nourish yourself.

Other relationships I Want to Strengthen   How/When
       Consistent for 2 Months: Yes or No   Result

Interests/Activities I am Willing to Try"   Dates Tried
       Consistent for 2 Months: Yes or No   Result

How I Will Create Meaning: Dates Tried
       Consistent for 2 Months: Yes or No   Result

Increase Non-illness Conversations/Interactions   With Who/When
       Consistent for 2 Months: Yes or No   Result

How I Will Get Support: Date Tried:
       Consistent for 2 Months: Yes or No   Result

Evaluating Results. Completing the Nourish Yourself Form is partly for awareness. Sometimes family members aren't aware how much of their conversation is about the consumer's illness or how difficult it is to not focus on that topic. The worksheet is also to encourage you to practice the behaviors. Sometimes people read and understand concepts but don't put them in practice. The worksheet focuses on two months because the first time you do any new behavior it will feel awkward which makes you want to give up and go back to what feels comfortable. In general, stick with the new behaviors for two months and your comfort will improve though probably the behaviors may still not feel natural. In four to six months you are likely to feel the full benefits of the new behaviors.

Real World Application

As hard as it may be, dedicating your entire life to your loved ones well-being is not helpful to you or your loved one. Finding ways to create your own meaning and find joy is important for your loved one as well as yourself. It's difficult to consider how your loved one's disorder may trigger unpleasant feelings in you. Of course you love her and want her to be well. Considering additional reactions may be hard. Are you angry at her for having the disorder? Are you embarrassed or ashamed that someone you love has a mental disorder? Are you avoiding your own life by dedicating yourself to hers? Has it become a way of not solving your own problems? Blaming your loved one for not having friends or not living your own life is not healthy for you or for her. If any of these issues are true for you, then face and accept them, then look at realistic solutions.

Completing this step may take some time, perhaps years. Keep working on it—it's worth it.

8 HOW SKILLS 4: BE CALMS

Managing your own emotions can be challenging. There will be times that you will be so frustrated with ineffective behaviors and intense emotions that you don't know what to do. The right decision may seem so obvious to you and you may still be angry or afraid that the consumer can't manage the right decision and instead follows a familiar pattern that leads to more suffering. You may be experiencing overwhelming emotion. At the same time you might have moments of excitement, when you see signs of improvement or a positive event occurs in the life of the consumer. Being overly excited may trigger feelings of shame on the part of the person with the diagnosis (They must have thought I was hopeless or I'm such a lost cause they're astonished I got a job interview). Excitement about progress can also trigger fears of abandonment, because getting better means other people don't have to supervise, help or take care of them as much. Being alone is one of the consumer's biggest fears. So while all emotions are normal and expected, you might wish to express them in a mild way. Turn the volume down! In these situations, BE CALMS is the skill to use.

Be CALMS

Be CALMS is about helping you regulate your own emotions in your relationship with your loved one. You won't always be successful in staying calm, but practicing these steps may help.

Be

Be is about being in the moment, being mindful. When you are in the moment and mindful, you behave gently even when being firm. You aren't bringing up past events or the history of the person with whom you are talking. In any interpersonal interaction you want to have a calm face and posture. Many consumers are reactive to body language and voice tone. Some are reactive to loud noises. Your being calm means you are not adding to the consumer's emotional overload.

71

Compassion

Remembering compassion is one way to help you remain calm. Perhaps think of the image of a third degree burn victim only the pain is emotional (Linehan, 1993). Then express compassion and validate the consumer. (You'll learn how to validate in Chapters 10,11, and 12.) Also have compassion for yourself. If you get frustrated with yourself, then you will increase your own emotional distress. Know that you too are stressed and you have struggled. Be gentle with yourself and compassionate about your own feelings and thoughts.

Accept What You Can't Control

Though we give you suggestions and ideas for ways to communicate more effectively with the consumer in your life, you cannot cure your loved one's illness and you can't keep him calm and you can't make him go to treatment or make a wise decision. When you go into any interaction with your loved one, remember the only person you can control is you. Then focus on your own words and choices, not those of your loved one. Trying to control what you cannot control creates anxiety and upset. This acceptance will help you remain calm and focused.

VaLidate

Don't lecture, defend, threaten or attack. Instead let the other person know that you get what they are experiencing and understand their thoughts and emotions (see the chapters on Validation). Remember that logic doesn't calm emotions. Lectures don't change the behavior of the consumer. Attacking the consumer or yourself only makes the situation worse. These behaviors are ways we try to control others but they damage relationships and make the situation worse. The intention may be to help the other person but the behaviors are efforts to control the situation. While it makes sense to want to control the situation, you can't control another person. These behaviors add to the distress of the other person, may increase suspiciousness and create an atmosphere of distrust. Often the person on the receiving end feels invalidated rather than helped. When someone is emotionally upset, the best strategy is to listen to what they are saying even if you don't agree with it. We'll discuss this more under Listening with WISDOM.

Be Mindful of Your Emotions

You may be so focused on your loved one that you aren't aware of your own emotions. Individuals with BPD are often quite in tune to your emotional state. They will sense your emotions quickly. When you are overly emotional, be aware and take a break, wait until you are calmer. The best decisions discussions, and problem-solving happen when people are calm. Your brain shuts down the planning and analyzing system when you become emotional. Be mindful of your own emotions. Recognize when you are no longer calm and stop until you can think clearly and be patient and open.

Separate and Slow Down

Very few situations are truly urgent. Taking time to think through a decision may lead to a better decision. Make a habit of saying "Let me think about it." That can save you from responding impulsively. If you routinely take breaks in discussions that are emotional, the breaks will become expected and normal. In addition if you are becoming emotionally distressed, disengaging from the situation is important. Because you appreciate the symptoms of BPD, when you separate you will give a time that you will get back together to discuss the topic. The same is true if you feel the consumer is speaking disrespectively or attacking you. Kindly state that this discussion isn't working for you and you will meet her in the same place in three hours to talk again. Notice that you say what works for you and don't tell her she needs a break to get in control.

If you do disengage, what do you do to get back in control of your emotions? You might take some time to do soothing activities. Then find your compassion. Remind yourself of the BPD symptoms. What symptoms is your loved one displaying? Ask yourself, what you are trying to control that is not in your control? Many times when we are anxious, sad or angry at someone it is because we want to control that person's emotions, thoughts, or behaviors. Once you've identified what it is you are attempting to control, then remind yourself of the goal of your conversation. Then focus on what is in your control that gets you closer to your goal.

SAVVy HOW SKILL: Be CALMS

1. **Be** mindful of your body language

2. **C**alm posture/calm voice. Remember compassion. Validate.

3. **A**ccept what you cannot control.

4. Don't **l**ecture, defend or attack

5. Be **M**indful of your own emotions

6. **S**eparate calmly if necessary. Slow the situation down.

When you find yourself becoming emotionally upset in an interaction take a break.

1. Give a time to restart the discussion. Own it as what you need not what the other person needs.

2. Soothe yourself. Drink some decaffeinated tea. Take a nap. Listen to soft music.

3. Remember compassion

4. Decide what you are attempting to control that is not in your control. Let it go.

5. State your goal in one sentence in terms that are in your control.

6. Focus on what is in your control.

7. At the stated time go back to discuss further or state you need more time.

Relaxation Techniques

When you take a break, relaxing your body helps reduce anxiety and stress which is helpful in being able think clearly and manage your emotions. In addition, relaxation is good for your physical health and helps decrease the physical consequences of stress. Different techniques work for different people. Some use meditation as a way of managing stress. You can also try guided imagery, rapid progressive relaxation, and breathing techniques. Living in a relaxed state takes practice so doing these exercises frequently will help you develop your skill.

Guided imagery. Guided imagery refers to using an imagined experience, directed by an instructor or a script to achieve a relaxed state. By using guided imagery to relax the body, your anxiety and stress will lessen. Guided imagery uses your senses to create an imagined situation and your body responds as though what you are imagining is real. It is much like imagining that you are holding a lemon in your hand. Picture it as a large, yellow lemon. You can smell the lemon and feel the roughness of the peel. Picture yourself peeling the lemon. The smell gets stronger and you see the white underside of the yellow peel. Now imagine that you take a bite of the lemon. Most people find they salivate when imagining this scene. That is an example of the body reacting as if something imagined is real. So imagining yourself in a relaxed place can help the body and the mind relax.

There are many guided imagery CDs available as well as downloads available online, including on my website. You can record your own guided imagery. The following is an example of guided imagery.

If you are comfortable doing so, close your eyes. If you prefer, just lower them. Settle in your chair, getting as comfortable as possible. Take a deep, breath, expanding your belly and keeping your shoulders relaxed, and hold it in for the count of six. Exhale, and repeat twice more. Then breathe normally, and focus your attention on your breathing. As you breathe, inhale through your nose and exhale through your mouth still expanding your belly rather than moving your shoulders up and down.

For the next few minutes, just focus on my voice. There is nothing else to do right now ,nothing to think about other than listening to the sound of my voice. Picture yourself dressed in comfortable clothes, laying on a recliner on a porch of a cabin. The cabin is surrounded by mountains and forests. Picture all your worries and stress rolling away from you, down the mountain, rolling faster, into a deep gulch. All your stress and worry is gone for the next few moments. You look around you. There are beautiful flowers in the yard. Just past the flowers are tall green trees. You hear birds singing. A stream flows nearby and you can hear the water gurgling over the rocks. A faint breeze cools your face.

The sky is a brilliant blue. A soft blanket covers you. You stretch your legs and let the recliner support your head, your arms, your legs—you sink deeper into the recliner.

You know you can stay here all day. The scent of an apple pie baking, or your favorite food comes from inside the cabin. You breathe in the scent.

Rapid Progressive Relaxation. Progressive relaxation is very effective in decreasing tension. To being, sit in a relaxed position. Let your hands rest loosely in your lap, or by your side. Keep your legs uncrossed. Close your eyes if you are comfortable doing so, otherwise lower them. Breath deeply in through your nose, all the way down into your stomach. Hold the breath for a count of three, and then exhale through your mouth. Breath in renewl, breath out stress. Breath in relaxation, breath out stress. Feel the stress leave your body as your breath flows out of your lungs.

Breath deeply again, filling your lungs. Hold for about the count of three and then exhale completely, emptying your lungs. Let the air flow out your mouth and take all your tension and worry out of your body. Feel your body begin to relax, feel your muscles being to let go of tension.

Take a third deep breath. Hold it, and then breathe out your mouth. Feel yourself relaxing more and more deeply with each breath.

Focus on your feet and toes. Now breathe in deeply through your nose, and as you do, gradually curl your toes down and tense the muscles in the soles of your feet. Hold your breath for just a few seconds and then release the muscles as you breathe out.

Focus on your calf muscles. Breathe in deeply and as you do, point your toes up towards your knees and tighten your calf muscles. Hold for just a moment, and then let those muscles go limp as you exhale. Limp like jelly.

Now breath in deeply, and tense the muscles in your thighs. Hold for just a moment, and then relax all those muscles. Focus on letting them go limp and loose.

Draw in a nice deep breath and gradually tighten the muscles in your buttocks. Hold this contraction for a few seconds, and then release your breath. Feel the tension leaving your muscles. Feel them relaxing completely.

Breathe in deeply and tighten your stomach muscles. Hold for a moment. Now release your breath and let your muscles relax.

Focus on the muscles in your back. As you slowly breathe in, arch your back slightly and tighten these muscles....Now release your breath and let the muscles relax.

Pull your shoulders up towards your ears and squeeze these muscles as you breathe in deeply. Now breathe out completely. Let your muscles relax.

Feel the heaviness in your body now. Breathe in again. Clench your fists and tighten all the muscles in your arms. Squeeze the muscles as you hold your breath...now release and gently breathe all the way out. Let your arms and hands go loose and limp.

Now tighten the muscles in your face by squeezing your eyes shut and clenching your lips together. Breathe in fully. Hold this for a moment...and now breathe out and relax all your facial muscles. Feel your face relax.

Take a deep breath in, and then open your mouth as wide as you can. Feel your jaw muscles stretching and tightening. Now exhale and allow your mouth to gently close.

Take one final deep breath in, filling your lungs completely...hold for just a moment, and then release and relax. Let all that air carry away every last bit of tension.

Take your time, and when you are ready, open your eyes.

Breathing Exercises. There are many different breathing exercises. Here is an example. Place one hand on your upper chest. Place the other on the abdomen with your little finger right above the navel. The goal is to breathe from the stomach, have the movement be in the stomach with very little movement in the chest. Breath smoothly. Slow your breathing. Breath in for 4 or 5 seconds and breathe out for 3 or 4 seconds. Alternately you can silently think pause, relax at the end of each breathing cycle(Barlow and Cerny, 1988). Slow breathing is one of the keys to staying calm and relaxed.

Practice Be CALMS

Think of a nonemergency situation that is very upsetting to you, one that you've become upset about in the past. Describe that situation to a partner. Your partner will role play with you and tell you the situation that is so upsetting. Your job is to use relaxation techniques and follow Be CALMS.

Practice the relaxation techniques on a daily basis. At the end of each day, rank your stress level from 1 to 10 with 10 being the highest level of stress you usually experience after a difficult day. Then rank your stress level after doing the relaxation exercises.

SAVVy How Skill 5: Practice

Learning new skills and interaction styles is challenging. Really challenging. There are whole books and theories written just on how people change. Think about your closet. Are your clothes grouped according to color? Or maybe according to purpose, such as work clothes and play clothes? Now imagine that someone moves your clothes around. All colors of shirts are randomly mixed together. Work clothes and play clothes are no longer separate. Think how you would react. What about your toilet paper roll— does it hang with the paper hanging or under the roll? Now imagine that someone turns your toilet paper so it hangs the opposite way. How difficult would that be for you? Most people report that these experiences would be difficult to adjust to. If we have difficulty changing the way the toilet paper hangs, imagine how difficult changing more complex, interpersonal behavior is!

Changing behavior and learning new skills involves more than understanding and observing. Practice is a critical part of learning something new and the step we are most uncomfortable with. Because practice is so important to learning, practice is one of our How Skills. Role plays are excellent ways to practice. Imagining yourself doing the new skill is an effective way to practice as well. Throughout the program we'll give you opportunities to practice the skills you are learning. We encourage you to practice on your own as well.

Real World Application

Individuals with BPD are usually tuned in to the emotions of others. When your emotions are added to the emotions of your loved one, the total emotional charge of the interaction increases significantly. When you are emotionally upset, that increases the emotional upset of your loved one and the emotions spiral upward. Though you may be focused on your loved one being able to control her emotions, the same is true for family members and friends. You may not be out of control and you may not be using self-destructive means to manage your feelings. At the same time being irritated, angry, or scared when talking with your loved one is not helpful and decreases your ability to think clearly and make good decisions. You may say that you are in control of your emotions with everyone but the individual who has BPD. That may be true. And learning ways to stay calm and grounded when interacting with your loved one with BPD is an important skill.

9   WHAT SKILLS 1: LISTEN WITH WISDOM

Fear seems to clogs ears. When frightened it's easy to miss the meaning of what someone is saying. Many times a person with BPD seems to have her own language as well and that increases the likelihood of misunderstandings. Learning to listen carefully, with wisdom, is the first of the what skills for parents.

Listening to daily activities is just as important as listening to problems and upsets. In fact, listening just as carefully, or maybe even more carefully, to routine interactions and events is part of listening with WISDOM. The individual with BPD needs to know she is interesting and that you pay attention to her apart from her disorder. For some the only way they know to get the nurturance they crave is through their disorder. Some families may think the individual who has a diagnosis takes so much time they want to focus their attention on other people when possible, but that may inadvertently increase the times the individual with BPD experiences distress.

Listen with Wisdom

Sometimes we think we've heard it all before or we think what is being said makes no sense so we stop listening. Listening with wisdom means we listen to truly understand. You also listen dialectically, to get the other person's truth even if you disagree.

Sometimes there is truth that is very difficult to find. It's like the story of the little boy who was in the barnyard shoveling through a big pile of horse poop. When his dad asked why he was shoveling the poop, the little boy replied, "With all this poop there's got to be a pony in here somewhere." Your job is to look for the pony.

W Willing to Use Listening Mind

Sometimes it's difficult to listen to information you have heard before or that seems similar to information you have heard before. It's difficult to listen to information that doesn't make sense to you. It's difficult to listen when you are rehearsing in your head how you can say No or attempting to figure out what the right response is. Willingness to use listening mind means that you listen mindfully. Your focus is on what is being said, regardless of your emotional reaction to the content.

I Invest Time in Understanding their Truth

Consumers have the symptoms of idealizing and devaluing and experiencing intense emotional reactions to events that can result in different views of events that happen. In addition consumers are not always the best judge of what they can cope with and what their skills are.. Linehan (p241, 1993) pointed out that even though the consumer may think in extremes, exaggerate and minimize, that is no reason to assume there is not truth in what she is saying. Listening for that truth is a skill. Being able to do so will improve your relationship and the communication between you.

S Remember the Specific Behaviors of BPD

When you listen and communicate with someone who has BPD, keep in mind that the person is likely to be suspicious and to fear abandonment. Someone with BPD is more likely to show emotional changes quickly and to devalue or idealize other people. Remembering the symptoms does not mean you correct your loved one, not at all. In fact, you will likely validate their thoughts. But remember the disorder influences their thinking. In addition, studies are showing that the hippocampus in people with BPD is reduced in size. This may mean that their memory is not intact. If you keep that in mind then it may help you have empathy when the consumer asks the same question repeatedly, has difficulty holding on to information you've given, or tells you the same story.

D *Don't Assume...*

she is okay because she looks calm

she can do something because she says she can

she can do something because she did it before (not under stress)

Individuals with BPD are usually excellent at masking their feelings. They may feel like they are falling apart on the inside and yet they maintain a calm exterior. Often consumers aren't good at knowing their own skills—they think they can do more than they can or underestimate what they can do. Sometimes they know how to do something but can't do it under stress. All that can be confusing to those who love them. When talking about tasks and expectations, be aware of these tendencies. Sometimes goals have to be adjusted based on trial and error. Remembering these facts may help you be more understanding when the consumer says she is going to fill out job applications and go to interviews, but doesn't. Understanding doesn't change your personal limits, but it may help you be less frustrated.

O *Be Open to Differences and Dreams*

When you listen to someone's hopes and dreams, be open to what they want to achieve. It may be that your son or daughter has not finished a single class but wants to be a heart surgeon. Listen openly. Maybe they will achieve that goal someday. If not, maybe they will finish college as a part of aiming for that goal. Discouraging someone's ideas is not helpful and can be invalidating. Maybe your daughter tells you she's met a wonderful man and he is unlike any one else she has ever met. You've heard that before. Just listen and don't judge.

What is important to your loved one may not be the same as what is important to you. Your values may not be same and what would upset you may not be the same. When you love someone with BPD, they will be passionate and intense about their beliefs. When you listen with WISDOM you listen with openness to their differences, a willingness to be mindful of their differences and accept them. At the same time be open to your own humanness. You will have negative thoughts and judgments even when you don't want to. You will want to control and protect when you need to step back and you will want to step back when you need to protect. Be aware of your humanness and be compassionate to yourself.

M Maintain Mindfulness and Compassion

People tend to treat others as they are treated, especially if we are in close contact with the person over long periods of time. We tend to yell at those who yell at us, be late to meet those who are late to meet us, give gifts to those who give us gifts, be sarcastic with those who are sarcastic with us and argue with those who argue with us. When you love someone with borderline personality disorder you may find that you are doing some of the same behaviors you notice in your loved one. You may call numerous times when she is late and ask lots of questions about what she has been doing. You may find that you begin to point out ways she falls short and raise your voice when she raises hers. You may refuse to answer her calls if she has refused to answer yours. Maintain Compassion and Respect is about remembering to act with respect and to manage your own emotions effectively even if the consumer is not.

Practice: Listen with Wisdom

Over the next week, pay attention to discussion you have with your loved one. Notice assumptions you might make and then listen carefully to see if your assumptions are correct or not. Write yes if you heard correctly and no if you did not. Regardless of the correctness of your assumption, respond with compassion and respect for yourself and your loved one. Over time notice how you feel differently when you talk with your loved one. You will feel more relaxed and accepting, less like you are going into battle.

Listen With Wisdom

Assumption You Made

Did You Check Out Your Assumptions?

Correct or Incorrect Assumptions

Compassionate Response

Real World Application

When someone we love is struggling with chaos, effective decision-making, and intense emotions to the point they can't seem to get their life on-track, naturally you want to give them advice and convince them to think and behave differently. Most of you probably have a strong urge to talk. Maybe you believe it is your obligation to tell them how to "fix" their life. Of course you feel an urgent need to help them be happy and to stop harmful actions. Yet a more important first step is to listen. Maybe your loved one isn't listening to you and are you listening to your loved one? True understanding is necessary before suggestions will be effective. No matter how many times you have heard certain ideas, stop interrupting and stop ignoring. Listen. Practice listening. You may feel uncomfortable, irritated and/or anxious with some of the thoughts your loved has. Keep listening. Listening is one way of connecting and improving your understanding. Listen to understand her point of view and how she sees the world even if you disagree.

10 SAVVY WHAT SKILLS 2 AND 3: DOUBLE CHECK AND BE CLEAR

Even when you listen with wisdom, you may not accurately understand what the other person is saying. When you double check you can be more confident that you're getting what the other person is trying to tell you.

SAVVy What Skill 2: Double Check

Double Check means to always check out if you are communicating clearly what you want to say and hearing what your loved one is intending to communicate. While it may seem uncool, it can save some heated arguments over misunderstandings. Taking time to double check can also slow a conversation down. That can help keep the interaction calm.

Check Out What Your Loved One Heard

Check out what your loved one heard you say. This is especially important when discussing issues that may be emotionally upsetting. Ask your loved one to tell you what they heard. If they didn't get your meaning, stay calm. No rolled eyes or aggravation in your voice, as that only increases the emotion in the interaction and makes it more difficult. Maybe you can tell them that was helpful. Don't blame the other person for not hearing right; instead take their feedback and consider how you can make your meaning more clear.

Check Out the Meaning of What Was Said to You

It's just as important that you understand the meaning of what the consumer is saying to you. "Are you saying…" is a way of doing this. Give your loved one the opportunity to listen to what you heard her say. The feedback may be helpful to both of you. You can do this casually so it doesn't seem stilted or like you are trying to be a therapist. Have a curious attitude, really wanting to understand.

SAVVy What Skill 3: Be Clear

So many times we think we are being clear but we aren't. Maybe we skate around the edges and hope the message was received. Maybe we don't want to be clear. Not being clear makes the situation worse in the long run. Expressing your limits doesn't have to mean being upset or angry or issuing an ultimatum. Sometimes it is simply stating what you prefer or how a behavior affects you.

Be Clear About Your Personal Limits

Only you can know what your personal limits are around financial support, behavior in your home, and the like. Once you decide what your limits are, it is important to be clear and consistent with what you are willing to give and accept. Your personal limits must be about what is in your control and what you are willing to do, not what you wish would happen. For example you can say, "I love you and you are welcome to live with me. I would enjoy the company. I also need you to let me know if you aren't coming home so I don't worry. Are you willing to do that?" You can say, "I will pay your rent for the next six months." You can say, "If you raise your voice, I will leave for a few hours so we can take a break." Those statements are clear and you can enforce them, if you are willing to. You can leave and you can pay rent for only six months and you can evict her if she doesn't let you know when she isn't coming home at night. You have to decide if you are willing to take the necessary actions to enforce your personal limits. If you aren't, then state the limit in a way you are willing to enforce it.

Relationship Based Statement of Limits

So what we've seen is that some of our personal limits are not in our control for one reason or another. Maybe no self-harm is very important to you, but the only actions that are in your control are not effective with no self harm. You have decided that you are not willing to kick your daughter out of the house for doing self-harm. So how does she have a personal limit about no self-harm? Some personal limits are relationship based. Relationship based limits means no action will be taken as long as the person is safe, but the relationship is weakened each time the action happens. For example, Nancy's daughter April uses her sexuality to get attention from men. April believes that having sex with men will get them to love her and believes that is all she has to offer. Nancy learns that April has another case of VD from another one night stand. Nancy has talked with April repeatedly about the dangers of promiscuity.

What is your natural reaction? Most people would wish April would behave differently. Most people would respond with shaming responses. Shaming someone is a way we have of trying to get people to go by the limits we believe they should follow. You might combine shaming and anger, upset that you've talked repeatedly about the problem and she is not listening.

People have rarely changed their behavior as a result of someone shaming them. They may externally appear to abide by the limits, but no internal change occurs as a result of shaming. Shaming is invalidating and leads the person to feel that they are wrong and not good enough and that leads to withdrawal and hiding.

Remember compassion? Have compassion for yourself. You must feel powerless, ineffective, ignored, and fearful for your daughter's future. It is understandable that you would want to control what you can't control, with the best of intentions, for her own well-being. Consider compassion for April as well. How awful it must be to want to be loved so badly and go about it in ways that just make you more sure that no one can love you.

The relationship limit would be to express your sadness that she has made such a decision. Be a little distant if that is what you feel. Then let it go. Remember that intense emotional reactions are overwhelming for the person with BPD and interfere with her ability to process information. Intense emotional experiences can also be a form of connection for people with BPD, a reassurance that you still love them and haven't emotionally abandoned them, even if the emotion is negative. Distance is less emotional and may be more effective in communicating damage done to the relationship. Do not overuse relationship limits and don't use them in a controlling way. Relationship limits are about communicating a genuine hurt that you feel.

Relationship limits are a response to serious behaviors that deeply affect your relationship with your loved one. You may be angry that she was rude to Aunt Alice, your favorite relative, but how does that compare with self-harm or promiscuous behavior? Relationship limits are used only for the primary behaviors that scare you and could involve safety.

Relationship Feedback

Relationship feedback is different from relationship limits. Relationship feedback means that you use Be CALMS and tell your loved one how her behavior has affected you. Using validation and My TALK, two skills that you will soon learn, will help you be effective in providing feedback. Relationship feedback differs from relationship limits in that you do not distance yourself or talk about the relationship being harmed. In relationship feedback you give your reaction. An example would be, "I know you did not want to come with me today to see your Aunt, and I appreciate how kind you were to her." Another example would be saying in a neutral tone, "I understand that you do not enjoy visiting Aunt Alice when she comes over. She is probably boring to you and you'd rather be with your friends. I wish that you could stay a few minutes before you go to your room or leave the house."

As you experience your limits in your interactions with your loved one, write them down on the following worksheet. Then consider how you want to express them

Personal Limits Worksheet

What limits are important to you?

What is in your control?

How will you respect your personal limit?

Are you truly willing to do that?

Be Clear About What You Can and Can't Control

Saying that you will give your loved one a monthly allowance but she can't buy cigarettes is not something you can enforce easily. You can't control what time she goes to sleep or how much coffee she drinks. You can't control how many boyfriends she has or what type of people she chooses to make friends with. You can't control if she decides to use drugs. Basically you can control you and you can't control her. You can control how much money you provide and how long you wait for her to show up when you've arranged to meet for lunch. So when you think about your personal limits think about what is in your control and not what is in her control.

Linehan (1993) has identified four options in any situation: Solve the problem, change your perception, radically accept or stay miserable. These options help you look at situations from a self-focused stance instead of trying to change someone else. If you radically accept the situation, sometimes it isn't in your power to solve the problem and changing your perception of the situation isn't helpful. Then living with radical acceptance of the situation as it is may be the best option.

Be Clear About Reasonable Expectations and Goals

The goals of your loved one must be the goals of your loved one, not yours. However, it is natural to have expectations such as getting a job, graduating from college, completing freshman year, paying bills when they are due and keeping doctor's appointments. But those are end result types of goals. Those goals may be completely overwhelming to someone whose emotions have made it difficult to finish a class. Such large goals may also lead to you and your loved one feeling discouraged.

Keep small goals in your mind. If your loved one is working on attending school, then maybe think about her being able to register. If her goal is to pay her bills on time, maybe think about her having a set place to put her bills as a success. Small steps are the way to success and by having smaller goals in your mind will help you see the progress that happens. If you are focused on her graduating from college, registering for a class will seem insignificant. In addition to keeping goals small, work on a limited number of goals at a time. Two or maybe three is plenty.

You may set goals for yourself, such as improving your listening or practicing validation skills. Be gentle with yourself as well and set small goals that lead to your larger goal. If you want to be a better listener, maybe your first step would be to not interrupt others when they are talking.

Goals of Communication

Sometimes you will have a set goal in mind for a conversation you want to have. Being clear about the goal will help you stay on target and not get sidetracked by other issues. Your goal may be to make a request, clarify a situation, ask for a change, ask for or offer help, build the relationship, understand better or to chat. Being clear about your purpose may help you not respond to conversational hot spots (statements that trigger a predictable response from you) and stay on track. For example if you want to have a relationship building chat, remember to not use that time to bring up problems that could derail the interaction. This helps to assure that not all interactions with the person you love are about issues she needs to improve or work on.

Be Clear About Your Response to Self-Harm and Know Your Emergency Plan

Families and loved ones understandably have difficulty with self-harm. Many become emotionally upset and use threats, often in an effort to stop the behavior. Unfortunately the result may be an increase in self-harm or your loved one keeps self-harm a secret. Keeping self-harm secret adds to the problem as could your reacting with lots of concern, worry, and attention. When someone is in pain, seeking comfort and nurturance can become a primary goal and understandably so. If you respond to self-harm with lots of nurturance, then that could become a way the person with BPD learns to use to help alleviate the emptiness she feels. A middle of the road response may work best. You may encourage the consumer to talk about what led to the self-harm. You get medical care if indicated or if you aren't sure and respond in a neutral manner as much as is possible. Encourage the consumer to discuss the issue with her therapist.

When in the midst of an emergency situation, it is difficult to think clearly. Having a general plan developed ahead of time may be helpful. Do not keep weapons or lethal amounts of medications in your home. Take suicide threats seriously. If someone is threatening suicide then an evaluation by her therapist or psychiatrist or hospitalization for safety is necessary.

Your crisis plan needs to fit your needs. Here is a sample crisis plan that you can adapt if you wish. You may not see the reason to include home address for example. In a crisis, sometimes your memory fails. I suggest you complete all information that you might need regardless of how well you know it. Complete this sheet with your loved one if at all possible

Crisis Planning Sheet

Name_____ Height_____ Weight_____

Home Address _____

Work Address _____

Home Phone _____Work Phone _____

Cell _____

Email _____Other: _____

License Plate_____ DL Number _____

Make and color of car _____

Emergency Contact(s)

Name_____ Phone_____ Relationship_____
Other contact information:

Name_____ Phone_____Relationship_____
Other contact information:

Name_____ Phone_____ Relationship_____
Other contact information:

Name_____ Phone_____ Relationship_____
Other contact information:

Individual Therapist

Name _____

Day Contact _____ After-hours Contact _____

Medications

	Name	Dose	Cautions
1.			
2			
3.			
4.			
5.			

Making Your Environment Safe

Access to Firearm: No Yes:

Access to Other Ways Harm Yourself: No Yes What?

_____

Methods to reduce access to these means until treatment can work:

Effective Coping Plan

What behaviors are a signal that you are becoming dysregulated?
1._____

2. _____

3. _____

What effective behaviors have you committed to doing instead? Only list actions that you are committed to doing.

A. _____

B. _____

C. _____

What are the signs that you are becoming overwhelmed with emotion?

A. _____

B. _____

C. _____

What coping skills can you use to soothe your emotions and stay emotionally regulated?

A. _____

B. _____

C. _____

D. _____

Who are some people you can call or places you can go for distraction or distress tolerance who do not know you are in crisis?

Name _____

Contact _____

Name _____

Contact _____

Place _____

Contact _____

Place _____

Contact _____

Who are some people you can call to help you stay on track? (You do tell them that you need comfort/support/feedback)

Name _____

Contact _____

Name _____

Contact _____

Name _____

Contact _____

7. Professionals who can help

Name _____

Contact _____

Name _____

Contact _____

8. My pros and cons for using skills to stay regulated and survive this crisis without making it worse (without digging my hole deeper):

Pros of Using This Plan   **Cons of Using This Plan**

Pros of Ineffective Behavior   **Cons of Ineffective Behavior**

Real World Application

People should just know how to behave in relationships, right? They should just know when they're pushing too much and at least they should be able to read your cues. After you've gotten upset a few times, then they should absolutely understand what pushes your buttons. Maybe those are thoughts that you frequently have. Individuals with BPD, while they can be sensitive to your emotions (when they are not overwhelmed with their own emotions) they are often not sensitive to social cues or the reasons for your emotions. They can sense that you are upset and don't connect your being upset with their behavior. Or their needs override that understanding. They may know you are upset that they have called fifteen times and their thought is if you would just answer they could stop calling.

Being clear about what you need in your relationship with the individual with BPD and being willing to repeat those needs and limits is part of having a successful relationship. You will need to state directly that you need her to not call after midnight or to not drop by without calling. Otherwise you will be upset and the relationship will suffer. For the individual with BPD your upset seems to come out of the blue. Really, they often don't read or understand social cues. Successful relationships are usually a challenge for anyone with BPD.

No one wants to think about an emergency occurring with someone you love. You probably hope that each crisis is the last one. After the crisis you are exhausted and drained and can't think about planning for the future. Yet having a plan can be one of your best actions to take.

11 PREREQUISITES FOR VALIDATION

Understanding what validation is an important first step. Though validation seems like a simple concept to understand, sometimes it isn't simple at all. In addition, understanding is not enough. Even when you can define and give examples of validation it is not always easy to be validating. Sometimes families and spouses get frustrated because they aren't successful with actually practicing validation strategies even though they understand them. One reason practicing validation can be difficult is because certain skills are prerequisites for learning validation, just like knowing how to read road signs is a required skill for driving or knowing how to measure ingredients is a required skill for cooking a tricky recipe. Sometimes parents didn't grow up in an environment that allowed or encouraged the development of these skills. Let's take a look at behaviors that are necessary for practicing validation. We've found the following behaviors to be critical to learning validation: Setting aside personal reactions, listening compassionately, and respecting and accepting differences.

Setting Aside Personal Reactions

Two observers of the same event rarely report the same view. You may have read the story about the blind men answering the question of what an elephant looks like. The man who is holding the leg says an elephant is like a pillar. The blind man who is touching the elephant's head says the elephant is like a pot. The man holding the tail says the elephant is like a rope. The impressions of the men holding the ear and the men holding the tusk are different from the reports of all the other blind men.

Your personal reaction to a situation is unique to you. Sometimes people will agree with you and sometimes they will disagree. People may feel similarly as you to an event or they may have different feelings. The key is that your feelings are yours. Every individual, due to age, temperament, past events, and perhaps interpretation may have a different experience.

Your loved one's feelings in any given situation are likely to be different than yours for many reasons--age, experience, genetics and social connections to name a few. Not wrong, feelings can't be wrong, just different. To validate your someone else's experience, you first need to identify your own feelings and perceptions so you can separate how you think and feel from your loved one's thoughts and feelings.

Being aware of your perceptions means you understand that your view of the world is not the only one and not necessarily the right view for everyone. Although you dislike a alternative music, prefer a conservative style of dress, believe in the superiority of the Democratic (or Republican) Party, and think meat is disgusting, others will not agree with you. Though someone disagrees with you, that does not mean either of you is wrong. You have different perceptions of the world and maybe different values as well. The tricky part of understanding different perceptions is recognizing that a different perception from yours is not necessarily wrong. We all believe our perceptions are right or we wouldn't keep them. Your perception is right to you and someone else's perception is right for them.

Setting aside your own perceptions means asking questions to learn what your child is really thinking and feeling. It's easy to assume that a consumer is happy or upset for reasons you think he is happy or upset. Sometimes that may not be the case.

Practicing Setting Aside Personal Reactions—Being Aware of Your Perceptions

Use the topics below for practice. Write your opinion about each.

Dating someone of a different race

Attending church (different from believing in God)

Guitars in church

Men with long hair

Dating someone twelve years older

Being overweight

Having a large house

Arguing to prove a point

Giving money to charity

Taking care of elderly parents

Tattoos

Living in the city

Living in the country

Clean rooms

Guests

Winning at sports

Family loyalty

Wearing all black

Forgiveness

Playing sports

Playing music

Cooking meals

Divorce

All A's in school

Able to win a physical fight

Having the "right" friends

Being the best

Politeness

Being the life of the party

Being popular

Boys crying

Girls crying

Physical beauty

Now go back and consider how someone could have a different feeling or thought about that topic. Are you able to accept a different feeling/thought without seeing it as wrong in an absolute sense, though it might be wrong for you? You may find some topics more difficult than others. Do you understand why it is more difficult for you to accept a different opinion on those topics? Do any of these topics that you have strong opinions about affect the way you interact with your child? Maybe you know other topics that you have difficulty accepting a different viewpoint. Add those to the list. Now go back and write how you think your child would respond to each of the topics.

How many did you think you knew? Sometimes we are so focused on communicating our beliefs and preferences to our children that we are unaware of theirs or even that they may have an opinion. People usually want their loved ones to agree with them on values.

Listen to what your loved one thinks and feels without considering your own reactions. Don't frown or smile when he responds, just listen and accept. Listen with an open mind, one in which you are wiling to understand someone else's world. Watch for facial expressions. Is he relaxed? Talking freely? Making eye contact? If not, then he may be trying to please you. If he agrees with every one of your opinions, even though you didn't say anything while he was responding, then it is likely he is parroting your beliefs and not thinking for himself or not comfortable expressing what he truly thinks. He also might not know what he thinks.

Setting aside personal perspective is most difficult when you have a strong emotional reaction. Perhaps your son wants to be a vegetarian and a member of People For the Ethical Treatment of Animals (PETA). You are an avid hunter and you love steak. To you being a member of PETA will mean your son will be left out of family hunting trips and may be ostracized by your friends. Validating his wish to be a vegetarian may be a challenge for you.

Perhaps your wife has a friend, who is very competitive, and successful in the business world. The competitive friend has a strong need to win and she frequently points out her victories to your wife. This friend keeps coming in bragging about her latest accomplished and this happens again and again. Perhaps when you were young you were tormented by someone who always seemed to win and bragged about her victories. This experience may have upset you and you don't want your wife to hurt like you did. You may be upset but perhaps your wife doesn't care. It is possible, really, that she simply doesn't care about her friend's boasting. Accepting that she doesn't care is validating her thoughts and feelings. Validating her feelings in this situation might be a challenge for you!

Setting Aside Roles

Setting aside your personal perceptions also means setting aside rules for what you think you must do as a parent, spouse or sibling. This is different from knowing your strengths and weaknesses. There are many roles people play in their relationships with others. Teacher, comforter, protector, caretaker, rescuer, blamer, cheerleader, lover, confidante, cohort, follower, leader, parent, policeman, geek, pretty one, smart one, mean one, assertive queen, lover, flirt, irresponsible on, sick one and more. These roles require different skills and different mindsets. Sometimes family members believe that if their spouse/child/sibling loved them enough, then they would not be depressed or would harm themselves. Some family members believe if they can't make the consumer happy then they aren't doing their job or the consumer doesn't love them enough. If you have a rigid view of who you must be and how the relationship with your loved one must be, this will limit your relationship and limit your ability to validate the consumer.

We all have an idea in our heads of what a good marriage looks like and what good parenting looks like and what our strengths and weaknesses are in being a spouse, sibling or parent. For example, you may see yourself as the playful parent who doesn't discipline or the disciplinarian who doesn't know how to play. You may see yourself as a good listener or as someone who doesn't have patience to care about your spouse's issues. Changing that view of yourself, believing that you can learn to use validation, will be important to being successful.

We may assign certain rigid roles to the consumer as well. A few possible roles include the following: the caring one, the fun one, the smart one, the creative one, and the athlete. The roles could be not so positive as well, such as the one who lies, the selfish one, the weak one, the sick one, or the problem person. If a person who never complains of being sick says he doesn't want to go to work because he doesn't feel well, we're likely to listen to him. But what if you someone who frequently complains of not feeling well complains of not feeling well and plans to stay home from work? As difficult and unnatural as it is, letting go of the role you may have put the consumer helps them also give up that role.

Reacting to others based on our past experiences with them is normal but may not be helpful. Reacting to others based on roles we've assigned to them for whatever reason means we may not really know their true personality. Be careful about preconceived expectations. With the possible exception of some emergency situations, the most important component of any interaction is validation of the consumer. Validation allows the consumer to develop who they are as best they can, separate from everyone around them.

Practice Giving up Roles

To practice giving up a certain view of yourself as a parent or spouse first recognize the role you have given yourself. In your notebook, write down what you think your role as a parent/sibling/spouse is. Rank order those tasks. Does the time you spend on each task reflect the priority you have given it? We want the time you spend to accurately reflect what you value in parenting. If having pleasant experiences with the consumer is a part of your role that you highly value, but aren't doing, give some thought to how you might change that.

Now how would you describe most of your interactions with your family? Are you serious all the time? Busy all the time? If you are usually silly and playful, spend some time being serious. If you are usually serious, spend some time being silly or playful. If you tend to be fast paced and always on the go, take two hours once a week to just be with your family with no agenda. The idea is practice stepping out of the role in your head and being with your loved one in different ways. You will likely feel uncomfortable not being in the role that you are familiar with. Doing this will help you experience how to step out of your perceptions and views to see someone else's views, a critical skill for validation.

Sometimes setting aside your personal reactions also means checking out the truth of a situation before responding. Just because he is the one who usually is at fault in a car accident doesn't mean he was the one at fault this time. Or because Melody has lied about her spending before doesn't necessarily mean she is lying this time. Allow your loved one the opportunity to change his behavior and not be stuck in a certain role in the family.

Family members of consumers often fall into certain reaction patterns. This means that you have a typical reaction that happens so often that your loved one can count on it. For example, let's say Chelsea knows that her husband gets angry when she buys new shoes. She knows it so well that she may have stopped paying attention to her husband's reaction. Imagine if you acted in another fashion, or if you did not react at all. You could get out of the trap you have inadvertently set for yourself in order to respond to Chesley in a genuine way, which may effect a greater change in her behavior. Or you may find a way to problem solve in a way that is more effective.

Setting aside your reaction doesn't mean you can't acknowledge it. Being upfront about reactions that you have can be respectful if done without judgment. Saying, "Look, I am keeping an open mind. But I have to admit that because you have lied to me before my trust in you has been damaged and creates some doubt. I am looking forward to rebuilding trust and I see this as an opportunity to do that." When you react this way, you give the consumer the chance to rebuild, to make a new decision and to behave a different way. You offer hope. You may do this many times before the consumer is able to take the opportunity and behave in more effective ways. Maintaining your belief that the consumer can make a different decision and not let past experiences define who she is important because it's about your attitude toward the consumer. Validation of hope and effort is partially dependent on your believing there is hope and on your ability to acknowledge small steps.

Letting Go of Shame and Guilt

Having compassion means that we are able to be vulnerable, accept that we are human, that we aren't perfect and accept that others aren't perfect either. Brene Brown (Lecture 2010), in her research on shame, talks about the importance of accepting and telling our stories. She believes it is through telling our stories that we get past the shame of not feeling good enough, smart enough, pretty enough, or anything enough. What helps us to accept our humanness, including our mistakes and our failures, is feeling the compassion of others. We are able to put ourselves into someone else's shoes and understand how they could feel the way they do. Accepting that others have different reactions than we do is one step, and one step further is to truly understand and accept the responses and reactions of others.

Shaming is the opposite of listening compassionately. Imagine that you and your wife are taking dancing lessons. She is having difficulty learning a step and is, in fact, not well-coordinated. She is flushed and biting her lip and you know that means she is feeling self-conscious. You notice others in the class watching you and out of embarrassment you make jokes about her dancing skills. Or maybe you say "What's wrong with you? This is so easy, why can't you get it?" Those responses are shaming statements and not validating. When you listen to her nonverbal communication in a compassionate way, you know that she's feeling not good enough. "Hey, you are so beautiful tonight. I am having so much fun with you. Learning these steps can be difficult for anyone, especially when you're being watched" is a validating statement, if you can say it truthfully. To listen compassionately you do not solve a problem or give an opinion. You listen to understand the other person's point of view.

Listening with compassion to your loved one's stories about what happened with friends, what happened at work, or at their volunteer job is an opportunity to help them feel validated and connected. Understanding how their experiences affect them is important.

Respecting feelings means that you believe that all feelings, and the expression of them, have merit. Many adults tend to discount some feelings as immature or silly. Sometimes feelings are judged as wrong or bad. The person who feels jealousy over a colleague's promotion may be judged irrational or selfish. People may question the values of a woman who is angry over the loss of an election for president of the garden club. Regardless of the reason for the emotion, people all have the same emotions, jealousy, anger, hurt, and sadness and emotions are important. The fact that different situations or events trigger these emotions does not mean the emotions are any less painful or important. The fact that the consumer's emotions are more intense, more reactive and of longer duration doesn't mean they aren't valid. Sometimes the most accepting people judge the consumer's feelings as fake or inappropriate because their reactions are more intense. Can you imagine someone telling you to cut it out, grow up or stop the drama when you are sad about losing a promotion or that a friend is angry with you?

Practice Listening Compassionately

Find a time when you don't feel rushed. Sit down with your spouse. Now just listen. If a little voice inside you starts listing the tasks you need to get done, ignore it. If you find you are judging this as a waste of time, ignore that too. Let go of any expectations you have for so-called meaningful conversation. If he doesn't talk at all, make a comment about something he is doing. If he jokes about what's wrong with you, just accept it and continue to listen. Your job is to listen. At this moment, nothing else matters but listening. This can be uncomfortable. If it is uncomfortable for you, stick with the uncomfortableness. Remember don't teach, don't interrogate, don't disagree, don't agree, just listen. Ask questions only to help increase your understanding of his point of view. Listen for a minimum of thirty minutes, no matter how little he talks.

Now summarize what your spouse had to say. As close as you can, describe his point of view. Repeat this practice once or twice a week for five weeks. At the end of five weeks you may notice some changes. Your spouse may talk more to you. You will not agree with some of the thoughts that you hear, but you will know more about what he truly thinks and feels which will give you the opportunity to validate him.

Respecting and Accepting Differences

Many times we treat individuals with BPD in ways that we would never treat our friends. We make fun of their ideas and share their secrets--many times because from our perspective they are cute. Perhaps your son has a crush on your best friend's daughter. You will very likely want to share this information and cute stories about his behavior with your friend. No harm done from an adult point of view. But your son will likely be embarrassed and wish he hadn't told you about his feelings. Respect is knowing how he would want his feelings treated and abiding by that, just because his feelings matter.

When a son wants to be just like his dad, that's flattering. It feels like he admires his dad and most parents want their children to look up to them. When a son is as different from his dad as black is to white, it can be difficult to accept. A son's different views and interests can feel like a negative judgment or even a rejection of his father. A father may believe it's important to have a group of male friends to go bowling, hunting or watch football. When his son prefers computers or reading a book, that can be difficult for the father to accept.

Imagine that your son is friends with a classmate who is not well-liked and you are worried that this friendship will damage your son's popularity. You don't see what your son sees in this classmate who doesn't seem to you to be a desirable friend. Accepting differences means that you accept your son's choice of friends and don't attempt to change his mind. This concept has proven difficult for many, many years. Many famous stories have been written around the theme of parents being unable to accept the choices their children make.

Accepting differences is the ability to understand that your loved one may have interests and may make choices that you would never in a million years even consider. It means not pushing your loved one to lead the life you live, or wish you lived, but letting them live the life that is right for them.

Practicing Respecting and Accepting Differences

Consider making a commitment to your loved one with BPD that you will no longer share any stories about your that they find embarrassing. You will respect their privacy. You will not laugh at issues that are serious for them. Think about the ways you have not respected them and make a commitment to not do it in the future. Write out your commitments and give them to your loved one.

For most everyone, there are behaviors, ideas, or interests, separate from the disorder, that they do not love about their spouse, parent, or friend with BPD. Some ignore these differences, some attempt to use reason to persuade their loved one to change, and some stay angry. What are those issues for you? Does your daughter want to be a singer ? Does your wife want to be a Buddhist? Whatever the differences that you find difficult to accept, spend some time putting yourself in their shoes and try to understand why they think/feel the way they do or what their experience is like for them.

Think of someone who has very different ideas than you and argues with you regularly. Then think of someone who listens to you even though they disagree. Think of how you feel in each situation. Think back to your own childhood. When you were 11, did you have views or wants that were not accepted by your parents? What about when you were 16? Describe what that experience was like for you. Remember that accepting differences does not mean agreeing. It means not demeaning or judging someone wrong for their thoughts or feelings.

Real World Application

In this chapter I discussed the prerequisite skills necessary to practice validation effectively: Setting aside personal reactions, listening compassionately, and respecting and accepting differences. Of cou course you want your loved one to share your values and your views—it's a way of connecting and seeing yourselves as being on the same team. Connecting and loving someone who has different beliefs, perhaps even beliefs that are the exact opposite of yours, is more difficult.

What I'm really saying is that relationships are more important than what someone believes or the way they think. Loving your spouse, child, friend or family member completely without any interference caused by differences in beliefs and viewpoints is a strong relationship. You don't have to agree or support their views. I'm asking that you accept the person and that their views and beliefs are theirs to have. This is very difficult to practice.

Over the next few weeks, listen to people who have different viewpoints than yours. Really listen. Maybe you listen to a conservative talk show commentator if you are more liberal in your views. Or maybe you have a friend who has very different views about religion that you usually avoid discussing. Listen with the idea of understanding and the goal of accepting the other person without agreeing.

12 WHAT SKILLS 4: VALIDATION

You've accepted the diagnosis, you have an understanding of why someone with BPD behaves as they do, you're taking care of yourself, and you're allowing yourself to feel your emotions. You're committed to learning, understand why it is important and are ready for the learning something new process, which is usually frustrating and difficult. Now let's address what validation is.

The What of Validation

One of the most important skills for family members of consumers to learn is that of validation. Emotional validation is the process of learning about, understanding, and expressing acceptance of another person's emotional experience. Emotional validation is distinguished from emotional invalidation, in which another person's emotional experiences are rejected, ignored, or judged. Validation confirms the worth of the person and that you understand their point of view has value. Validation helps build a sense of identity, facilitates emotion regulation, and is a tool for positive interpersonal relationships. Sounds perfect for someone with BPD, right?

Validation means that you acknowledge your loved one's point of view as being valid even if you don't agree. It means you acknowledge their point of view even if you disagree 100% and can't see how they could ever think like they do.

Marsha Linehan (1997) has identified six levels of validation:

Level I: To be present. This means that you are listening to what your loved one is saying, not thinking about your golf game or wondering how long before your loved one gets angry or thinking here we go again. You are mindfully listening to what she has to say. You don't interrupt or try to talk over her or think about your arguments against what she is saying. You listen without judging.

Level II: Accurate reflection. This means that you summarize what your family member has told you. Don't do this in a sing-song manner or a fake therapist-like voice. Really summarize to be sure you have understood what she is saying. If you don't have the meaning correct, and this will likely happen a surprising number of times, then listen again. "So you're upset that your friend didn't call."

Level III : Guess. Based on what your daughter has told you, you might make a guess that she is feeling hurt or devalued by your not being in town for her birthday. Remember that only your daughter knows how she feels. If she says that is not how she feels, then you must accept it. Also, if you are using this level of validation, frame your guess as a guess, which acknowledges that you don't really know. You don't include explanations or why they shouldn't feel the way they do, you are just guessing how they feel. "So I'm guessing you were really scared when that happened."

Level IV: Validate the person's behavior in terms of causes like past events. Linehan's (1997) concept of Level 4 validation is an important addition. Sometimes behavior is understandable and normal only when we consider what has happened in the past. A man who screams at the sight of a bird may look silly unless you know he was attacked by a bird a few months ago or when he was a child. Once you consider that past event, his present behavior makes perfect sense. "Given your experience with birds I totally get why you were so scared."

Level V: Validate the person's behavior in terms of present events and normal reactions. Linehan (1997) sees this level as important to helping people know what is normal. We've all wondered at some point or another if we were normal. This level of validationis about giving feedback about normal responses. To be sad when a pet dies is normal. To be angry when a friend wrecks your car or flirts with your girlfriend is normal. To be scared when you are taking a very difficult, important test, to be hurt when you aren't invited to your friend's party, or to be sad when you aren't accepted into the college of your choice are all normal emotions.

Level 6: Radical Genuineness. Linehan (1997) uses this level to address the importance of authenticity in an interaction. No one can ever know exactly how someone else feels That is true. Sometimes though, we've had shared experiences. We've been there. Perhaps it's the experience of losing a parent. Every person's relationship with their parent and the way they feel grief is unique, but there is still universality in the experience. When someone says they miss their mother who has died, you may know that feeling well. Many people know what it's like to be teased about appearance. Letting yourself be vulnerable with another person and sharing truth even when it is unpleasant is Level 6. Radical genuineness is also just being genuine in the interaction, one person to another.

So basically what you are doing when you validate someone is listen, find the truth in what they say, and acknowledge the truth and/or acknowledge your acceptance that they feel or think the way they do regardless of whether you agree or not.

Linehan says validation is an acceptance strategy. Acceptance can help someone manage their emotions more effectively when they are in an emotional state. Whenever your family member is having difficulty managing her emotions, use validation. Do not attempt to tell her how she should do things differently or suggest any change in her behavior when she is upset.

Now that you know what the levels are, let's look at them more closely. Level I isn't really hard, it's just that we forget. We live in such a rushed world that it seems like such a waste of time to just listen to someone and not be doing something else at the same time. To do lists, friends, television, chores and work, are just a few of the daily competitors for your attention. If your attention is important to the consumer though, she will learn how to get it, though she probably is not be aware of what she is doing. Usually people listen when consumers are upset. So not validating the existence and the importance of the consumer by being present and listening may result in the consumer being upset. Level I means we must listen mindfully, and only listen. So maybe it's not hard to understand but is a challenge to actually do.

Level II isn't so hard either really. If you listen to what someone is saying, you can summarize their meaning, at least what you think is their meaning. The difficulty is, once again, time. Conversations go much slower if you are summarizing what someone else is telling you. At least it feels that way. If you avoid a misunderstanding it may actually be faster in the long run. Another difficulty is that our own emotions get in the way. We hear something that we think is ridiculous and we react. We don't stop to check out whether what we heard is what someone meant, we just jump in to tell them how wrong they are and to defend ourselves. Accurately reflecting what the other person said would go a long way to help them feel heard and feeling heard is sometimes the most important issue for people with BPD.

Level III is a little more difficult. Sometimes people with BPD can't identify what they are feeling. That's an issue. Putting a name on an emotion helps manage the emotion and knowing what you are feeling helps you choose a coping skill to help deal with the feeling. So using Level III helps the other person identify and label emotions. Your job is to be a willing guesser. That means you keep an open mind about what the other person is feeling and don't judge their feeling. Remember to not argue with the person. If they say they are not scared, then they are not scared.

The important point about Levels IV and V is to not use the wrong one. If a feeling or thought is a normal feeling that anyone would have, then validate it as normal. Never validate a normal feeling by saying it's understandable because of what someone went through in the past. And don't validate a thought/feeling as normal that is understandable only in terms of someone's past.

The What and How of Validation

Validation

What Skills	How Skills
Listen	Mindfully
Discern Truth	With Acceptance
Acknowledge	Authentically

The What of Validation

If you look at the six levels of validation, you'll see that the "what" to do is to radically listen, discern the truth of what is being said, and acknowledge the truth. For example if someone says they hate someone you really like and know that they liked just a few days ago, then you can say, "Right now you really hate him and you believe you'll hate him forever. That might be exactly what happens."

Notice that these two sentences don't mention agreeing with the person, because in this case you don't agree with her. You are hearing and acknowledging what is true for her. You can't validate someone if you aren't being mindful of what they are saying or doing and that means it's not about what your thoughts are. Remember that mindfulness means to be completely and fully in touch with the present moment in a non-evaluative way. Just listening to someone mindfully is a validating action.

The second What of validation is to discern the truth. Let's say that your spouse is angry with his boss who he usually respects and admires. He says, "That man is a total jerk. He only thinks of himself." You know the man and you don't think he is a jerk. You also don't think your husband will think so when he calms down. Discerning the truth means that right now your husband thinks his boss is a jerk and you actually don't know for sure how long he will think that way. You also know that he is mad at his boss. So

114

instead of saying, "You're just mad," or "Don't you remember all that he has done for you," which is not his truth right now, you say "You are so angry at him. I don't think I've seen you this angry with him before."

The How of Validation

First of all you can't validate someone if you aren't being mindful of what they are saying or doing. Remember that mindfulness means to be completely and fully in touch with the present moment in a non-evaluative way. You aren't just listening, you are listening mindfully, which is a validating action in itself. The second how of validation is to do so with acceptance. If you don't agree with what someone is saying, showing that disagreement through your body language or tone of voice is not accepting. Accepting is respectfully acknowledging someone else's feeling/thoughts as valid regardless of whether we agree or not. Thoughts and feelings are just thoughts and feelings and every human being has their own thoughts and feelings. Non-acceptance closes people down emotionally and doesn't help them learn from their past choices and only leads to the feelings becoming more intense.

Authentically means that you find a way that you truly believe in what you are saying and that you truly accept the person's thoughts and feelings. Pretending won't work. The way you interact with someone is influenced by what you truly think and believe in ways you aren't aware.

Some Guidelines for Validation

The value of validation is that it communicates acceptance. To be effective, the meaning behind your words must be acceptance. For the meaning behind the words to be that of acceptance, it is important that you find a way to feel that acceptance. Remember, acceptance doesn't mean agreeing, approving, supporting or encouraging any actions or ideas. No way. It only means that you accept that what the consumer is thinking or feeling is her internal experience and that is neither right or wrong, it just is.

Validation of what someone is thinking or feeling doesn't mean you accept inappropriate behavior. It may mean that you understand the feeling or thought that motivated the behavior and you can see how feeling that way could lead to the behavior but it doesn't mean you agree with the behavior or accept the behavior. Someone's thoughts and feelings are always validated though not agreed with while inappropriate behavior is not validated as appropriate, though you may understand the reasons the person behaved as he did. Thoughts and feelings are always validated. Behavior is not always validated. If someone is angry and hits the person he is angry with, the feeling is validated but not the action. You may validate that you can understand his wanting to hit, but hitting is not appropriate.

Just as you don't validate inappropriate behavior, you also don't validate what isn't true. If your daughter is angry with her therapist and says "She never helps me. I'm worse off than when I first saw her" and you know this isn't true, you DON"T say "You are right, she never does anything to help you and you've made no progress." You can say that you understand that she thinks that way, but you don't say it's true. To validate the truth you would say, "You think she never helps you and believe you are no better than when you first started." If she asks what you think, you say "I can see how you would think that way because lately you've had to deal with some of the same issues you had when you first started. As for me, though, I've seen some changes." You can then give details about those changes in the spirit of pointing out what you have observed, not to show her she is wrong.

Validating Progress or Characteristics

Angela is a 23-year-old female who has dropped out of college three times because of incapacitating depression and difficulties with relationships. After two years of therapy she has successfully completed a semester at the community college. Her parents were so excited and happy for her they took her to dinner to celebrate and bought her a gift. They thought they were validating her progress when they said, "You've accomplished a big step toward recovery." Angela became upset and refused to attend the dinner. She claimed she wasn't returning to college for the next semester. What happened? First, remember that validation is about validating the other person's truth. Angela didn't think she was on her way to recovery. She'd struggled to complete the semester and wasn't sure she could do it again. So when her parents validated the behavior she'd shown, completing the semester, she felt invalidated, that they didn't understand how difficult the process had been for her.

Sometimes you can authentically validate a characteristic that you appreciate in someone and get a negative reaction. You validate what you see as the truth and do so authentically and yet your loved one will become upset. That could be confusing. Validation is not supposed to result in someone being more upset. What happened to validation valium? There are several possible reasons. One is that the acknowledgement that your loved one is getting better is scary to her. That may make no sense. How could she not want to get better? To get out of the hell she's been in? Getting well is a new, unknown experience that involves loss in addition to gains. Getting well means less help from others, maybe less attention from her therapist, and others will expect more from her. She may worry about having to get a job and maybe give up relationships with fellow consumers. All that can be overwhelming and she's likely to be unsure she can do it.

Sometimes invalidation happens because your view of the person is not the view they have of themselves. Imagine that Jamey, a thirty-two year old consumer, carries groceries to the car of an elderly couple. You've noticed that he's done other helpful tasks and you say, "You are a kind person." Jamey becomes upset, "No, I'm not." You are astonished because throughout your relationship with him he has acted in kind ways. People have some set views of themselves. They may see themselves as good athletes or a people person or an introvert. Certain views of themselves become part of who they believe themselves to be. When that happens they only accept information that fits with that view. In Jamey's case he believes he is a selfish person. Any information that contradicts that view is discounted. Not only that, but the person usually feels like you don't really understand him or know him. So validating a characteristic that you see as true but the person doesn't accept as true about themselves will likely feel invalidating to the person. Sometimes the only way you can learn what characteristics the person doesn't accept about himself is through experience.

Validation and Saying No

No is a little word that is so very challenging to say. 'No' is a key to the first step, which is setting limits. Setting limits is important for preventing compassion burn out and for communicating effectively with your loved one. There's no way around it, you'll have to say no and mean it. You have to take care of yourself and set your own personal limits Think about it. When was the 1 last time you said no to the consumer in your life? What happened? Most likely you were punished in some way for saying no, though probably not intentionally. No one likes to hear no, and people with BPD have very intense feelings. Combining validation with setting limits may work better. So here's the no equation: Validation + direct no + laid back manner + owning it.

Validation Equation

validation + no + laid back manner + owning it

How you say no matters. Remember validation? Validation needs to be part of any "no" statement or any interaction that could be distressing to someone with BPD. Validation is verbal valium, helping to calm everyone, not just those individuals with BPD. Usually, one of the most important facts to validate when you are going to say no is to validate that you love and accept them, to counteract their interpreting that you are saying no because you don't care about their feelings. Of course they may still think in that way, but repeated experiences and your reassurance may decrease the intensity of this reaction if not immediately then over time. Another area to validate is your understanding of the importance of their request to them.

Saying No

How many different ways can you think of to say no? You can hint, be direct, sugarcoat it and avoid it. Let's look at some ideas about saying saying no effectively.

Be matter of fact, but clear that you mean it. History matters too. What has been your pattern in the past with saying no? That history will affect how your no is accepted.

Here's an example to show you what I mean. Jane, who had dropped out of college twice, talked about her wish tom reenroll in a university in the Fall. She lived in the southwest and hoped to return to a college in the Northeast. Her parents had told her many times they would not support her going back until she had passed some courses at the local community college, which she did not do. Her parents met with her with their family therapist and told her they would not pay her university expenses because she had not met their requirements. Jane did not seem that upset when she told me this. I asked about her reaction and she explained, "Oh, that's not their real no. That's just their maybe no." Sure enough, Jane returned to college that Fall. So even with the simple No, family history may change the meaning of the word. So think what your real no is like. Start using your "real No" and drop the "maybe no.

When you say no, own it. No one can really argue with your feelings. So instead of saying, "You wouldn't really like that," say "I don't want to do that." Some other examples include:

I appreciate your thinking of me, that was kind of you, and I regret that doesn't work for me right now.

I know you are eager to go shopping and I want to take you, and I cannot go today. How about tomorrow?

I understand this is important to you and you feel like it has to happen now. Though I want to help you, I am exhausted and cannot do it today.

I love you, and I don't agree with you.

I want to say yes to you because I know you want this, and I can't because it's not in the budget we agreed to.

Another characteristic of an effective no is to be clear, no waffling words. "I don't think so," leaves room for argument. "I do not agree," is more difficult for someone to argue with. No one can tell you what you agree with or don't agree with. At the same time the saying of no may go best if said softly, with love.

No is a difficult word for many individuals with BPD to hear. No matter how well you say no, there will be no angry reaction. Using validation does not mean the no will be accepted with no outbursts. But over time, using validation should help the consumer to not react so strongly and see no as a rejection of them or as a failure to get what they want. It offers acceptance of the person while at the same time setting limits.

While saying no may be difficult, not saying no is more difficult in the long run. Your loved one may be upset if you say no, but if you avoid saying no, she will be much more upset when she has believed you would say yes and then at the last minute did not. Being willing to say no when you need to protects your relationship in this way as well as by protecting you from burn-out. Setting limits and speaking up about unacceptable behavior is more difficult when you have allowed the behaviors to go on for a time than it is to set the limits the first time the behavior occurs. Though more difficult, you can still do it. Speaking up doesn't mean repeatedly telling your loved one that you will tolerate their abusive behavior while your loved one reams you out. Let's look at an example.

Robert had an anger problem. He repeatedly yelled at his father, cussing him, and hitting the wall with his fists. He blamed his father for his lack of success, saying his father never supported him, never believed in him and always criticized him. He also blamed his father for his parents' divorce when he was eight years old. His father feels guilty about the divorce and knows he was critical when Robert was younger, so he nods his head and apologizes, over and over. Robert's behavior doesn't change. He often becomes enraged at his father when he experiences failure or disappointment. Robert believes that his father is responsible for his lack of success and Robert's father believes he deserves Robert's rage because of the divorce. Robert's father isn't helping Robert by not standing up for himself. In fact, his taking the blame may actually help Robert avoid taking responsibility for solving his own problems. Avoidance of important issues in life usually creates more emotional dysregulation. Avoidance of issues and setting limits is different from arguing and making the situation worse. Walking away when someone is too upset to listen is a step toward not making things worse. Being wise about choosing the time and place to talk about difficult subjects is important and avoidance.

Self-Validation

Validation is like relationship glue. Validating someone brings you closer. Validating yourself will help you accept and better understand yourself, which leads to a stronger identity and better skills at managing intense emotions. Validating yourself will also help you better manage your own emotions and that will lead to your loved one also being more in control of her emotions.

Being out of control of your emotions is a painful experience and damaging to relationships. Knowing how to self-validate is important to learning to manage your emotions effectively. Self-validation means you can accept your internal experience as understandable and acceptable. But learning to self-validate is not so easy. How do you apply the six levels of validation to self-validation? Notice that mindfulness and self-validation go hand in hand.

Level 1 Be Present

To be mindful of your emotions without pushing them away is consistent with Linehan's first level of validation, to be present. To be present also means to ground yourself and not dissociate, daydream, suppress or numb your emotions. Being present means listening to yourself. Feeling the pain of sadness, hurt, and fear is most challenging and difficult. At the same time avoiding emotions results in quite negative consequences, while accepting allows emotions to pass and helps build resiliency. Being present for yourself validates that you matter and that you have the strength to feel.

Level 2 Accurate Reflection

Reflection means to make manifest or apparent. For self-validation, accurate reflection is acknowledging your internal state to yourself. Perhaps you reflect on what triggered the emotion and when. Maybe you reflect on the ways you feel the emotion in your body and consider the actions that go with the emotion. Reflecting means observing and describing, components of mindfulness. When you observe and describe your internal experience, you do not interpret or guess or make assumptions. You would say, "I feel angry and it started yesterday after my wife cancelled lunch. I sense tightness in my stomach, so maybe there is fear as well."

Saying, "I am a total loser as a spouse and no wonder my wife doesn't want to spend any time with me," would not be stating the facts of your experience. Stating the facts of your experience is validating and helps build trust in your internal experience. Interpreting your experience in ways that you cannot observe to be true invalidates and leads to distrust in your internal experience and more

Level 3: Guessing

Sometimes you won't be sure what you are feeling or thinking. In these situations you may want to say something like, "If someone else were in this situation they would probably feel sad. Am I sad?" You might also guess by looking at the actions you want to do. If you want to hide, maybe you are feeling shame. Maybe you are thinking shame thoughts. You can notice where you feel body sensations, such as fear is often felt in the throat. If you are feeling fear, maybe you are thinking scary thoughts. Guessing your emotions and thoughts based on the information you have will help you learn more about yourself.

Level 4: Validating by History

Sometimes you will have thoughts and feelings that are based on events that have happened in your past. Maybe you are afraid when your loved one becomes sad or gets in a relationship. Validating yourself by saying, "It's acceptable and understandable that I am afraid, how could I not be afraid, given that in the past she has had difficult times in relationships?" Validating your feelings means recognizing your feelings and accepting them. Then you can decide how to express them appropriately, if at all.

Level 5: Normalizing

Everyone has emotions. It's normal to feel sad, angry, hurt, ashamed, or any other emotion. Getting angry with your loved one is normal. Being afraid for her is normal. Having emotions that you aren't proud of is normal. Recognizing your emotions and accepting them will help you not act on them in ways you might regret.

Level 6: Radical Genuineness

In terms of self-validation, this means being your real self and not lying to yourself. It means that you don't pretend to be someone you aren't. Rejecting who you are is one of the highest levels of invalidation. An important distinction is that who you are is different from what you do. You are not your behavior, yet changing some of your behaviors may alleviate some of your suffering.

Self-validation is one of the critical steps for living with intense emotions. It is part of forming relationships and thriving. Practice and more practice will help you self-validate automatically.

Practice

In the following scenarios, choose the comment(s) that would be validating.

Part 1

1. Conrad comes home with his head shaved. He informs you that he's vegan now and will not eat meat and won't wear leather because of the torture that animals endure.

    A. "This is just because of that new girl you met. Every time you get interested in a girl you take on whatever they believe in. I'll give you two weeks and you'll be eating hamburgers again.
    B. Don't expect me to cook anything different. I do enough around here.
    C. You've always loved animals and cared about how they are treated.

2. Lukas came home from a job interview for a computer company. He says even if he gets the job he probably won't take it because he doesn't think he can do what the job requires. If his mother wants to validate him, which of the following could she say?

    A. Sounds like it's a complicated job and you're worried you won't be able to do well.
    B. You always look for excuses and this is just one more.

C. You are so smart, you can learn. You'll do great.

3. Lesley scheduled an appointment with her tutor. On the morning of the appointment a friend cancelled their lunch plans. Lesley is crying, fearing that she's lost the friendship. She says she can't make the appointment with the tutor.

   A. Of course you can go to the tutor. Your friend just cancelled lunch, she didn't say she didn't want to see you again.
   B. Stop overreacting
   C. How disappointed you must be. And scared. I know you cherish your friendship.

4. Amanda told her mother that she was panicked about driving to school.

   A. Seriously? Get a grip. It's a piece of cake. You stay on the same road the whole way, don't even have to turn.
   B. As smart as you are you'll have no problem at all.
   C. You have to make a big deal out of everything. I can't do every thing for you.

5. Jake's father learned that Jake had lied about filling out job applications. Jake explained how ashamed he was that he was 24 and hadn't finished school or ever held a job. Which one of the following statement would probably be validating to Jake?

   A. You're just lazy. You'd say or do anything just to sit on your butt all day.
   B. Of course, I should have thought of that. How awful for you! No way should you have to go through that.
   C. It's hard to be a beginner, especially when you feel that you are behind others your age.

6. Marissa is screaming cuss words because her mother told her that her boyfriend cannot move into their house.

   A. I can see how important this is to you.
   B. Keep it up and you won't live here either.
   C. You must really care about him.

7. Jennifer is upset because she didn't get accepted into the college she wanted to attend.

   A. It will be okay. Don't get upset. You'll end up liking another college even better.
   B. I told you to take the study course for the entrance exams so you can't blame me.
   C. That must be a huge disappointment.

Part 2

The more you practice validation the more natural it will be. Over the next two weeks, practice using each of the levels every day. Yes, every day. Check off your practice below. Also record the results.

Mon Tues Wed Th Fri Sat Sun   Result

Level 1

Level 2

Level 3

Level 4

Level 5

Level 6

Part 3

What level of validation would you use in this situation?

Jillian is a 28-year-old female with borderline personality disorder who is trained as a nurse. She currently is keeping house full time. Her husband Todd is a real estate broker. Jillian feels abandoned when Todd is at work, especially when he works at night or on weekends. Because Todd has asked her to stop calling him at work. Jillian is certain he is cheating on her, though there is no evidence that he is. She complains to Todd. "I know you're seeing other women. You would rather spend time with her than me, wouldn't you?"

What level of validation would you choose?

Level I is not likely to be effective by itself. If Todd listens very closely, giving her his full attention, but says nothing, then she will likely escalate, because in this situation she is asking Todd to tell her that she is important to him and that he loves her.

Level II would be saying "You're feeling that I don't want to come home because I'm seeing other women?" Then Todd could add, "You are the only woman I want to spend time with."

Level III Guessing that she is feeling neglected could help. "I'm guessing that you're feeling neglected because I've been working a lot and I've been so busy I haven't been able to talk with you on the phone as much as before."

Level IV "Because men stayed away from home and cheated on you before we got married, of course you would think I am doing the same. It makes perfect sense that you would think that."

Level V "I am away from a home a lot. I've had a lot of work to do with people transferring here for work and I've had to show a lot of houses at night and on the weekends. I haven't been able to spend much time with you. Anyone would be upset and most wives would wonder if I was really working."

Level VI: "I truly understand how upsetting it is for me to be working away from home so much. It is a change that I don't like either."

Now go back and practice self-validation using the same work sheet. Practice for two weeks.

Real World Application

If there was one skill that I could urge you to learn, it would be validation. Validation helps the individual with BPD develop their sense of identity, manage their emotions and be able to problem solve more effectively. Validation strengthens relationships. You have to get past the point where you are awkward using it because it's a new skill. And you have to persevere through your loved one chiding you about what new technique you are using. When you use it naturally and frequently, it will improve your communication with those you love and be a strong support for your loved one in her recovery.

Chapter 13 What Skill 5: STOP Invalidation

Everyone who knows me knows that I drink too many soft drinks. I've stopped and started too many times to count. It's a really bad habit that I have and some of the people in my life have noticed and commented. For example, I'll get a soda from the refrigerator at work and one of my office mates will put her hands on her hips, frown and say, "You don't *really* want that." I know where she's coming from. She knows that five minutes after I finish that soft drink that I'll be groaning about why I keep drinking sodas. It doesn't matter that I know the reason she's saying it though. I still react in the same way. I get a little bit angry. I mean of course I want it. I just took it out of the fridge didn't I? And I'm an adult. I can drink a soda if I want one. Her next statement will be something like, "You know it's not good for you." If I didn't like her so much I'd want to scream. Of course I know it's not good for me. Drinking soda is not logical. But my behavior is not about logic. Clearly. She's trying to help but her actions don't encourage me to stop drinking soda. Her actions encourage me to hide my soda drinking from her and to be angry with her. How did her helpfulness go wrong? She invalidated me.

Emotional invalidation is when one person communicates to that your emotions are unreasonable or irrational, or should be hidden or concealed. Emotional invalidation occurs when a person's internal experiences are rejected, criticized, ignored, or judged.

Haim Ginott (1988), who was a famous pioneer and leader in the education field stated this: Primum non Nocere. It means first do no harm. What does that mean to you? Maybe it means your family member is safe and protected when with you, that you are a safe person. You want to provide a protective, safe emotional environment for recovery. How do you do that?

An invalidating environment goes against what families and loved ones want to do. Invalidation is emotionally dysregulating to most people and particularly to people with BPD. When you don't have a secure sense of who you are, then you look to other people to define you. Many consumers look to their families. Validation is one of the most important keys to supporting a consumer because it both facilitates the development of a sense of self and provides a safe environment for recovery. A very powerful technique but one that appears too simple to have the impact that it does. Perhaps because of its easy-to-understand quality, emotional validation is often overlooked. Surely such a challenging disorder as BPD needs a much more complicated intervention. The truth is therapy for BPD is more complicated than offering emotional validation. But emotional validation is a key factor and it is one of the most important steps family members and loved ones can take to support and encourage recovery from BPD.

On the surface, validation is a technique that most people believe they already do. In fact, most families would argue profusely that they are validating . However, once they learn exactly what validation is, they are shocked to recognize that not only are they not validating but sometimes they are invalidating the consumer.

When a person feels out of control of their emotions, they usually do not feel confident. They are shaken, uncertain, and grasping for safety. When we tell someone who is upset how they should or should not feel, we are likely lowering their confidence and increasing their feeling of being out of control of themselves. Consider this example. At noon your daughter is sobbing, claiming that her boyfriend hasn't called today and he always calls by noon. She is sure this means he is breaking up with her. You point out that he could be busy or maybe he left his phone somewhere. She keeps sobbing and saying she knows the relationship is over. You finally say she is overreacting and there's no reason to be this upset over one missed phone call. Perhaps you go on to say she is going to drive him away with her neediness if she doesn't stop, just like she has done before. There may be some truth in what you say, but you've just told her that her thinking and feelings are wrong. Though you are trying to help and don't want to see her in such agony over a missed call, you are telling her to not trust her own thoughts and that she needs an outside source to tell her the truth.

People who are repeatedly invalidated may become confused by the criticism of others. They may see themselves as not fitting in and being different. They may fail to develop confidence in their emotions, one of nature's most basic survival tools. They may develop patterns of behavior to defend themselves against feeling so confused and overwhelmed by the differences between what they know they feel and think and what others are telling them is the right way to feel and think. Let's discuss some of the patterns we have seen in our practice.

People Pleasing

One of the ways people adapt to invalidation is by becoming a people pleaser. Some children become hyper alert to cues from their parents as to what is the right thing to say and feel. They may choose a career or a college major to please their parents. They may outwardly agree with their parents on politics, use of drugs, or the right friends to have even that though they don't really have that opinion themselves. As children they abided by the rules and gave their parents no trouble. Some continue to adulthood in the same way and parents are mystified when they may a suicide attempt or are arrested for shoplifting. They may have a secret life and not really be the person their parents think they know. Others rebel openly in high school, maybe doing everything their friends want them to do (pleasing their friends). When parents invalidate their children's thinking, one reaction may be that the children don't tell their parents what they think and they may not develop an ability to know their own beliefs and thoughts.

Agreeing with the opinions of others opinions reduces the likelihood of rejection. Most people fear rejection and find it painful so if agreeing with whoever is speaking or whoever is the most important person in your life helps reduce those painful feelings, then it works in the short run.

When an action works to reduce unpleasant feelings, then it is likely that that action will be used again and again. But there are too many people to please for this strategy to work well. What pleases one person doesn't please another, so the people pleaser can never find the right way to be, he is always wrong. He is so focused on trying to get the "right" response he may lose the ability to even know his own feelings. Turning to others to see the right way to think, feel, and behave, a strategy which may worked for him as a child when he just pleased his parents and perhaps his teachers, works against him as an adult.

Some people pleasing children are rewarded with attention, praise, or gifts when they are seen as doing well in school, dressing correctly, winning contests or achieving some other criterion, but the bar is stringent and perfection can never be obtained. No matter how well they do, family members, often with the motivation of helping the child, see a way the performance could be better.

Some people pleasing children have people pleasing parents who are focused on a façade of perfection—having the perfect family, the perfect outfit and the perfect life. This façade of perfection automatically generates invalidation. You can't show the outside world any shortcoming in yourself or your family. You must look fine. This is very confusing to children who know the family is not fine. Mistakes and missteps are tragedies of shame in this family in particular, yet perfection is of course impossible.

The Rebel

A different way of coping with an invalidating environment is for the consumer to protect herself by rebelling, giving her family an in-your-face I don't care attitude. In our experience the Rebels really cares a lot but they're angry that they feel put-down, controlled, or rejected by their family and/or friends. In their minds they have no chance of being good enough for others so they don't even try. In fact they often do the opposite of what people they care about want. This behavior may start as a way to express their feelings of anger but can become a lifestyle and a part of their sense of who they are. The Rebel is likely to choose similar friends in high school, or worse be a loner and see his fellow students as being similar to his parents.

The Hopeless

Some individuals with BPD may try to please their loved ones but nothing they do works. The grades are never good enough. Their friends aren't the right friends and their thoughts and choices are stupid or lucky. This consumer gives up and becomes withdrawn and perhaps passive. The hopeless child loses faith in himself. He doesn't see any point in taking any action because he doesn't see the connection between his actions and the results. Working hard does not result in success or anything good enough. The consumer who has given up hope of his parents' acceptance may become depressed (Seligman,   ).

The Scared

Some children respond to invalidating environments with fear—fear of being wrong, fear of someone's mood, or a generalized fear that they don't understand. Unpredictable environments, where the parenting style changes without warning, can contribute to a child being scared most of the time. He's on alert because he never knows when his behavior will be acceptable and when it will not. He stays on alert, ever vigilant for cues that his environment may change. He grows up and continues with the same pattern.

Consider the daughter of an alcoholic mother. When her mother is sober, the mother is connected and validating. She listens, she helps with school work, and organizes play dates. The daughter is emotionally safe. When her mother is drinking, she throws things and screams, scaring her child. This child lives in fear, waiting for her mother's mood to change. She learns that her world is unpredictable and not connected to her own actions. She learns to live in fear and her view of the world is unquestioned in her adult years. She may not even realize how she came to be afraid of life.

The Angry

Anger can be used as a shield from hurtful comments and disappointments. Hostility is difficult to overcome and many people begin to avoid the individual who seems angry all the time. That can be lonely but the risk of being hurt or humiliated is too great. Giving up anger is difficult as it is effective in many ways, such as motivating others to be more careful with their words.

The damage done by invalidation is not set, but falls on a continuum. Consumers develop a style of interacting with the world such as the categories we discussed above to protect themselves and to try to fit in, belong.. In our experience, the more consistent the invalidation the more damaging it is. Even mild invalidation may significantly damage a biologically vulnerable individual, one born with a strong tendency to emotional dysregulation. Children who are biologically hardy (tougher emotionally, more resilient) may be minimally affected by emotional invalidaton.

Part of emotional health is being able to manage and regulate your feelings, as discussed above. R.D. Laing, MD, a psychiatrist, said that when we repeatedly invalidate people or deny their internal experience that we make mental invalids of them. Invalidation that denies someone's experience and states that another view is really true can make a person feel crazy when they are not. In some families invalidation can be so extreme as to create a double bind for the child. If he believes his own experience and says that his family is unhappy and argues a lot, his parents will be angry with him, punish him and withdraw affection. If he goes along with the idea that his family is happy and fine, then he is denying his own reality and feelings. Validating a consumer's feelings is an important step for overall emotional growth. If you don't validate the feelings, how can you help the child learn to express, cope, and accept and problem solve? The child must be able to observe his feelings and express them to be able to manage them effectively. (Steiner, 2003). Validation is also an important step for healing, a critical part of recovery that you as a parent or spouse can provide.

When family members learn about validation and invalidation, they often look back with concern, recognizing the invalidating comments they may have made over the years. No one can do what they don't know how to do or even know is important to do. The importance of validation, to the best of our knowledge, has primarily been recognized since Dr. Linehan wrote about validation in 1993. Going forward with new skills is doing the best that you can do and that is all any human being can do.

Practice Changing Invalidating Statements

Over the next five days, notice invalidating statements you make to others and to yourself. Record the statement and the feeling you had when you made the statement. Then rewrite the statement to a validating one.

I. Invalidating Statement to Others

How You Felt

Change to Validating Statement

II. Self Invalidation Statement

How You Felt

Change to Validating Statement

III. Invalidating Statements by Others

How You Felt

How You Responded

Real World Application

I believe that invalidation is to your loved one's emotional recovery much like nutritional deprivation is to physical health. You can stop one of the major issues for someone with BPD by learning about invalidation and being aware of when you are invalidating. You can learn to validate and to repair the situation when you inadvertently invalidate, which will happen. Of course other people will invalidate her. And by changing your invalidating statements and actions to validating ones, you will still contribute an important part to her recovery.

Invalidating statements and actions often precipitate emotional storms for the individual with BPD. Such statements and actions also are likely to support the lack of trust the individual with BPD has for her own thoughts and emotions.

Validation supports the development of the mindfulness, both of the world and of your loved one's internal experience. Thus the individual with BPD is able to see interactions with others in a more objective way. She's also able to use emotional input in a helpful way. With less emotionally distorted information he is able to make better decisions. This relationship between mindfulness and validation seems transactional as well. Validation supports the development of mindfulness and mindfulness is necessary to validate self and others.

14 SAVVy What Skill 6: My TALK

If you have taken a skills training course, you know that DEAR MAN is one of the interpersonal skills (Linehan, 1993). You can use that skill, along with GIVE and/or FAST instead of My TALK. The steps in My TALK are below:

My   **My point of view**

T   **Identify the facts (Double check if emotional interchange)**

A   **vAlidation then Assert your feelings, limit or question**

L   **Listen with WISDOM, Double check and validate**

K   **Keep to one point at a time**

My point of view: Start with the facts from your point of view. Keep it simple and try to keep limit it to around five sentences. When you give too many details, people stop listening. If this is an emotional interaction, then Double check (is what you said what she heard). Did she hear what you were trying to say?

Validation. Once you have communicated clearly your view of the facts, then you validate the consumer. Validate what is true to you and do it in an authentic way. You might validate your understanding of her behavior in the incident you are discussing. If you are searching for something to validate, consider validating that she listened carefully.

Assert your feelings, personal limit or ask a question. Then ask for feedback or assert your limit or request something from the consumer. "I know that you are tired of not having a car and it's very difficult to ride the bus in this city. My guess is you are pretty frustrated even trying to figure out the bus schedule. But I think this program is helping you and I'd like for you to stay committed to it for another week, until you finish." Remember to not ask questions that you already know the answer to. Try to limit your statements to 2 or 3 at a time. That makes the information easier to process for someone who is emotionally upset. It also means she knows she will get a chance to speak soon and may have less urgency to interrupt or dispute a point. That means she may be more likely to listen instead of forming her responses to you and attempting to remember what she wants to say.

Listen with WISDOM, Double Check and Validate. After you listen with Wisdom, double check the information you heard. Did you hear correctly? Validate the other person's point of view. Validation communicates understanding and acceptance which is particularly important if the interchange is about a difficult subject.

Keep to one point at a time. Sometimes when communication is going well, you may want to discuss all issues that you can. That often backfires because the consumer gets overloaded with information and then the communication that was going well becomes difficult. Or once you begin discussing something that is important to you, you may feel internal pressure to keep talking, to release the feelings you have kept inside. Sticking to one point at a time will be more effective.

Practice

Practice having conversations about pleasant events or neutral subjects. Maybe talk with about a play you saw last evening and share with her that the main character reminded you of her because she had a good sense of humor and could make others laugh.

Share the guidelines with a friend or family member. Practice using the guide about different situations with that person before having the conversation with your loved one. Maybe practice telling your loved one you are going on a trip for two weeks or that you cannot loan him the car today.

Real World Application

Staying on track when having a difficult discussion with someone who has BPD is difficult. Having a guide to follow can help you focus on the one issue you wanted to discuss, not six million issues over the past twenty years. Reading the guide and understanding it is easy. Practicing it is not so easy and many times it may help conversations go better but it will not take all the conflict or emotion away.

15 SAVVy How Skill 5: Practicing SAVVy

One of the important parts of practicing new skills is being accountable.
Below is a n example of a simple card to track your progress.

There is a blank line under Willingness and Acceptance for you to add which
part of that skill you are practicing. Blanks are also under the skill of Taking
Care of Yourself so you can list what lyou will do. Under the days of the
week mark if you practiced the skill or not.

Parent/Friend Practice Card

	Mon	Tues	Wed	Thurs	Fri	Sat	Sun

Skill

Willingness /
Acceptance of

_____

Taking Care of Self by

_____

Taking Care of Self by

_____

SAVVy

Taking Care of Self by

_____

Be Calms

Set Your Intention

Listen With Wisdom

Double Check

Be Clear

Validate Others

Self-Validate

My TALK

139

16 What Gets in the Way of Doing What Works

No matter how many times you have told yourself you will not lose your temper or you will not rescue your loved one, you probably find yourself doing just that or some other behavior that you've promised yourself and maybe a therapist that you absolutely, positively will never do again. Why is that? First of all, it is difficult to make changes. Anyone who's tried to give up fast food or exercise more knows that. And then there are other reasons. Let's take a look at some of the issues that will make it hard for you to do what works in place of what doesn't work.

Fear

Though what you've been doing hasn't worked so well in the long run, it is familiar and you can probably pretty much predict what happens. There might be chaos, but you've been through it before and somehow it is less anxiety producing than doing something new. When you behave in a different way, you don't know how your loved one will react. That can be scary. It feels safer to just keep doing the same behavior.

There's evidence this is true. We know that when a person is used to being reinforced (having something pleasant happen) for certain behaviors, he will go to extremes to get that reaction to happen before he gives up. This means that if you've been giving money to your loved one every time she overspends, then she will expect that behavior to continue. If you stop, then she is likely to do whatever she can think of to get you to continue. She will do what she can to get you back in the familiar pattern that is positive for her.

Going through the super-sized chaos will feel like the situation is worse because it is worse. And that may be what scares you, the situation getting worse. Unfortunately, your fear is valid. The behavior you want your loved one to give up has to get worse before it gets better. What you want is extinction of the behavior, that she will no longer demand money from you and better that she will budget so she has enough money to pay her bills for the month. What you will get first is a strong reaction aimed at your changing your mind. Maybe before you said no your loved one cried and made statements about being so stressed and worried about her bills that she couldn't get out of bed, couldn't go to therapy. Maybe she misses a therapy appointment or two or more before she lets you know. If that's the before, then the after might be that she quits therapy altogether, stops taking meds, loses her job or stops paying rent and is evicted. At some point you are most likely to decide it isn't worth it and go back to giving her extra money when she asks for it. She calms down and the same behavior pattern continues.

She is simply following a behavioral rule that applies to us all. When a behavior that used to be reinforced is no longer reinforced, they the behavior becomes stronger before it extinguishes. It's up to you to draw the line where you are comfortable and problem solve as to how you can set the limit and stay in your comfort zone. If you are not comfortable with her being evicted, then pay her rent directly to the landlord as part of the support you give her, not as extra money. Then stick to your decision about not giving her extra money. The good news is that if you are consistent the behavior will change.

Change is Too Hard

Learning new ways of interacting can be so discouraging. Change is sooooo hard even with the best of intentions. Remember to take small steps and reward yourself for practicing. Have I mentioned how important it is to practice each of the skills? I can't emphasize that enough. Don't aim for perfection and practice, practice, practice. Soon you will find you are automatically responding in different, more helpful ways.

Believing You Can Solve the Issues

Maybe asking for help is difficult for you. Maybe you believe the family should take care of its own. For whatever reason, you want to solve the problems for your loved one on your own. Because people with BPD are often witty, funny, smart and charming, it's easy to believe that they could be that way all the time if the right person loved them enough or if they had no reason to fear being abandoned. This can be a seductive belief. But BPD is an illness that requires treatment by specialists. Loving the person with BPD is important but that is not the answer for recovery. Sometimes the consumer avoids therapy by convincing those who love her that they are the ones who can help her. Consumers sometimes say they will not cooperate with a therapist and won't tell the therapist anything about their lives. They might make that choice. But professional treatment by trained therapists is necessary for recovery.

Win Lose View of Relationships

Some people look at interactions with others in terms of win-lose. If you are discussing where you want to go for vacation or what you want to eat for dinner, then winning would be that your preferred option is the one that is chosen. Win/lose means that the other person apologizes when there is a disagreement. Win/lose means that regardless of the strain it puts on the relationship you push your own point of view.

This type of relationship is also about being right and not being wrong. Some people have great difficulty acknowledging they are wrong about any subject. They care more about being right than about saving the relationship.

If you tend to focus on win/lose right/wrong interactions, you will find it difficult to do what works for your loved one with BPD. Acceptance that the consumer may make decisions you don't agree with and may have opinions and feelings that you don't understand is necessary in a healing interaction.

Emotion Contagion

Emotion mind (Linehan 1993) is when your thinking and your behavior are controlled mainly by your emotions. Logical thinking is not part of emotion mind. If you are typically in emotion mind, then you will find it difficult to be helpful to your loved one. If you are sad because of the stress your loved one is enduring or angry because of the behavior of your loved one, you will be focused on your own experience and have difficulty functioning in a healthy way or in a way to provide safety and comfort to your loved one.

Many family members find themselves emotionally dysregulated whenever their loved one has a difficult day. It is completely understandable that you would be emotionally upset when someone you love is depressed or angry or otherwise emotionally in pain. At the same time sometimes your emotions may be controlled by our loved ones emotions. It's like you catch her emotions. If you are an emotionally sensitive person, it is likely that you would be strongly influenced by her emotions and then be unable to use the skills we've discussed. Finding a therapist to help you build a healthy way to not "catch" your loved one's emotions would be helpful.

Not Understanding the Science of Behavior

Rules of behavior say that whatever follows a behavior and increases the likelihood the behavior will recur is reinforcing to the behavior. The only way you can know what is reinforcing is by the individual's response. You go to work and you get rewarded with a paycheck. That may be reinforcing for you—it is for many people. But some people go to work because they enjoy the work itself. For them the paycheck is not the reinforcer. The work is. If you have a pet, you know that treats are reinforcing. Most animal trainers use treats in teaching new skills. Humans are no different. We like doing things that are followed by rewards we like.

Some people respond well to praise and want to work harder when they are praised. Sometimes people do not like praise and stop working when they are praised. Giving praise is not always reinforcing. Sometimes your attention can be reinforcing. If every time your daughter has a problem you rush to her side and give her lots of understanding and then when she is doing well you take a rest, not giving her any attention, it may be that whenever she wants your attention she will have a problem. This can become a cycle.

What is reinforcing can be puzzling. Sometimes your getting upset is reinforcing to your spouse or child who has BPD. Though it may not make sense to you, individuals with BPD are clear that indifference is the opposite of love and your showing anger means you still care. People with BPD are usually quite sensitive to what upsets you and know just the right words to say to push your buttons. If you respond, she knows you still care, that you have not abandoned her. If you don't respond, she may fear you no longer love her and try harder to upset you.

When your daughter shows improvement, you may be very excited. Perhaps you are hopeful that she will no longer suffer as she has in the past. You want to encourage her so you tell her how happy you are and how wonderful it is that she is doing so well. Then you are surprised to and disappointed when she regresses. Many times consumers can become frightened by doing too well. They are fearful of success for many reasons, such as abandonment, high expectations of others, and the unfamiliarity of doing well.

Real World Application

Making progress toward improving communication is a challenge. You will encounter difficulties and roadblocks. Sometimes you will think you are making progress and sometimes you will not. You may be tempted to say nothing works.

Problem solving is a challenging process and there will be times that it seems the changes you are making are not making any difference. It's easy to get discouraged and give up and that's often a reason that progress isn't made. If you are struggling, ask yourself if you are truly practicing the ideas outlined. Are you practicing enough so that they become a part of your natural way of living your life? Is it accurate that there have not been any improvements? Think back many months ago—what were your interactions with your loved on like before you started this program?

Has enough time passed? Change is often slow. Are you looking for the improvements that you can truly expect? In a brief period of time such as six months, you can see changes in the ways you interact and communicate. This doesn't mean that your loved one will be calm and happy, though I wish that could be the case. Even if you don't see major changes, are there changes that you can see that are improvements over the way your interactions went before you started this program? Be careful about giving up. Slow progress and small changes add up.

17 Self-Validation vs Shame and Guilt: Getting to the Solution

Jim and Diane Hall

Two potent emotion states hover over the family members and more pointedly, the parents of those who suffer from borderline personality disorder. These states are represented by the words **Guilt** and **Shame**.

Abject suffering is clearly the burden of the large population who has the symptoms of BPD. Their paths to recovery are difficult, painful and challenging. And…they do not suffer alone. Close family members and friends experience their own distinctive pain, confusion, self-blame and helplessness. All of these and other negative feelings are exacerbated by the personal lived experience of guilt and shame.

In simplistic terms, **guilt** is defined by some as "One being responsible for wrong-doings". **Shame** is a more personalized internally experienced conviction of "I am a bad, hopelessly flawed person". Or, "Guilt is What I Did" and "Shame is Who You Are" says Brenee Brown.

Comingled, these two beliefs are a deadly combination for all of us who have deep, caring feelings for our ill family member. Plus, we are often met with spite, suspicion, and even accusations of wrong-doing by many in the mental health profession, the general public, and even within the confines of our own family units. We have experienced stigma and without proper education, feel helpless.

Usually, one hears these two words together "feelings of guilt and shame". However, in the world of mental illness, **guilt** is most often a point of torment within the realm of **family shame** is more often mentioned in descriptions of the pain of **those who suffer**.Wikipedia says **guilt** is a state in which one experiences conflict at **having done something** that one believes one should not have done and it is closely related to the concept of remorse, or conversely, having **not done something** one believes one should have done. Interestingly, it also states that "When we see another person suffering, it can also cause us pain. This constitutes our powerful system of empathy, which leads to our thinking that we should do something to relieve the suffering of others. **If we cannot help another, or fail in our efforts, we all too often experience feelings of guilt**. People who are more prone to high levels of empathy-based guilt may be likely to suffer from anxiety and depression."

Broucek states in Wikipedia, that **shame** may occur in any situation of embarrassment, dishonor, disgrace, inadequacy, humiliation, or chagrin. Utterances like "Shame!" or "Shame on you!" by others regardless of one's own experience or awareness, may also contribute to a "sense of shame". Parents, take heart. The environment is a mine field full of embarrassment and humiliation especially for a deeply sensitive child. Peer insults, names on the board, exclusions from groups or gatherings, targeting from the cyber-world.... church, school, work – daily encounters, all have the propensity to impact feelings of shame.

Wikipedia continues with a quote by Helen B. Lewis, Psychoanalyst, "The experience of shame is directly about the self. In guilt, the thing done is the focus." Also quoted are Fossum and Mason saying, "Shame is a painful feeling about oneself as a person, while guilt is a painful feeling of regret and responsibility for one's actions." These feelings universally occur in reaction to a myriad of difficult mental and physical illnesses but they certainly do not facilitate the recovery of the loved one or the well-being of the family.

For decades, parents and caregivers have been blamed as the source and cause of mental illness. Society points a menacing finger at parents whose children display overt perplexing behavior in public – notes come home from teachers, birthday party invitations are absent, displays of uncontrollable emotion and destructive aggression bring prospects of shame and erosion of self-worth to the loved one spilling over to the family who is supposed to "fix it". Every incident of exclusion or consequences from unacceptable behavior further erodes self confidence in the person who is genetically susceptible – and the mountain of shame grows and grows. "We MUST have done something terribly wrong" the parents say – (silently at first, as none wants to admit that might possibility be true). Jim and I began to blame one another for our children's frequently misunderstood "unacceptable" behaviors and actions. The seed of Guilt is planted. And it too, grows and grows.

Dr. Blaise Aguirre, Director of Boston McLean's 3 East BPD Adolescent Unit, states that "Two thirds of our patients who have been treated for BPD at this unit do not have a history of abuse. We have observed these families to be well-intended but in some cases mismatched to their children." This statement makes a lot of sense particularly when one thinks about how mismatched many couples are…in our case the mismatch was glaring. It took many years of living and eventual outside help to reach the nearly impossible "50 yard line"! Mismatched couples are probably in the majority when one looks at the national divorce rate – how can parenting be deemed a "matched" relationship at the get-go? Raising a grounded family is a huge challenge, an enormous responsibility, a priority, an honor, a foundation of infinite love – and an honest "team" approach. A pretty tall order in today's fractured and splintered society.

In family units, the behavior of each person reflects upon the others. "You're a member of this family." "You represent the whole team." "You belong to this church." When the mystifying symptoms and behaviors of BPD appeared during adolescence at our house, chaos reigned. One by one, the pins fell. Unacceptable behavior reflects on others, shame radiates with each slip, we all begin to hide, to isolate. The isolation hinders support. What do you say when asked how the "kids are doing?" What do you write in the family letters at the holidays? Hopefully, many of us will find support in NAMI or DBSA or MHA, or NEA-BPD (or all!) but in the meantime the struggles continue – **shame** and **guilt** grows for both the one who suffers as well as the family.

Mom's Story

The teen years for our kids were chaotic – excelling at school – erratic at home. Traveling father, mother in school or working. Alcohol was the respite for the parents and the source of problems for the kids. College years were bumpy but both successfully graduated. Dad still traveled; Mom was working. Alcohol become more of a respite for Mom, and more problematic for the kids. One child sought counseling on campus and was given the diagnosis of depression. Careers began. Jobs came and went. Unexplained, instantaneous emotional reactions escalated. Relationship breakups were particularly crushing for our children. Our loved one was 23 when life became unmanageable and within days, Jim signed the papers for inpatient psychiatric care - diagnosis: bulimia.

While in treatment, we would talk on the phone and encouraged full disclosure of family life, school and social experiences. About two weeks into treatment, the shoe dropped, "Mom, I am concerned about your drinking." Well, I was concerned too. Since the kids left for college, Jim still traveled, and although I had rewarding work during the day, the nights were longer, and some nights I couldn't remember at all. The conversation continued, "I want you to be around for a long time…" I was shocked and pushed off the cliff into reality. "I promise to do something about it" I said. I sat dazed for several hours – flooded with fear, shame, guilt, waves of uncertainty (how or could I stop?) – a Mom, a teacher, an alcoholic?

That night, Jim gently shared his deep concern and offered support. I decided to be evaluated at a treatment center and the answers came back, affirmed. I was an alcoholic. One of the counselors asked if I had broken any bones from falls – no – had I been arrested – no. "You will" she promised, "if you continue." So with Jim's help, we began.

The years churned on. Both kids struggled with their working and personal relationships. One continued in outpatient therapy and a substance abuse program while juggling a full time work schedule. Then a suicide attempt requiring five days in ICU and psychiatric hospital lock-down for six weeks – diagnosis: bipolar with hypomania. At least, in sobriety, I fortunately had the capability to listen, process, worry, lose sleep, and stagger under an ever growing bag of guilt for my own out of control drinking in their growing-up years. I had not set a good model. We kept up the perfect family image for the work and social community and now I fully acknowledged the dysfunction at home. And I had been a contributor.

Ten turbulent years passed. Jim and I retired and tried out "leisure living" – golf, travel, church work, visits to the kids – one married with two little ones by now. Then the other shoe dropped. A highly experienced therapist finally diagnosed borderline personality disorder. This was shocking to all of us – a

DBT treatment program was recommended but our loved one would not consider treatment at that time. By this time, my anxiety and depression had become unmanageable so I sought out a psychiatrist who understood BPD. She prescribed medication and an excellent psychologist to help me. I saw the psychologist the next week and within an hour was at the bookstore to buy Dr. Marsha Linehan's book and workbook for Dialectical Behavior Therapy. By the way, I've been seeing the same psychiatrist and psychologist since 2001 and they have been valuable beyond words – to both Jim and myself.

A few months after the BPD diagnosis, our loved one made a household move for a job in an idyllic resort setting. Having just left the comfort of a home of 13 years, familiar security and stability crumbled. The new job was a disaster. The closest treatment center with some knowledge of DBT was 90 miles away but the 180 mile round trip for three months was faithfully completed. Unfortunately, there was no family program to involve Jim and myself.

The next year was very taxing for all of us. Jim and I made over 100 calls all over the country looking for programs with intensive and in-depth dialectical behavior therapy. We talked with 60 admissions counselors and decided on three with the best reputations who might even partially accept our insurance. We sat down with our loved one and presented written information on all three and asked for a careful review and consideration and to make the choice. We pledged our love and support.

Then we found NAMI, the National Alliance on Mental Illness. Immediately they signed us up for Family to Family and the class started the very next week. I went alone the first time. I came home and raved about the people, the stories like ours, the diversity of the group – and that it was being taught by two men! Jim joined me the next class and he's been an active advocate, supporter, and participator ever since.

What kept us from NAMI all those years of turbulence? My therapist mentioned it but the shame and guilt and denial that "things will get better" postponed our decision to walk that walk. When things got totally unmanageable and desperate for us – we found this door. Yes, at first it was hard to get there and get the door opened, but we always felt better upon leaving than when we arrived. There were all kinds of programs to help us –

support groups almost every night of the week, classes, speakers, and friendships that can thrive in an environment of acceptance. We were trained to lead support groups and teach Family to Family. This part of our lives plus the guidance of my therapist – has saved our marriage and preserved our family unit. This is the point where hope entered our lives.

Our loved one chose an intensive DBT center in a large city in the northeast and continued treatment there for three years. Remaining there for ten years now and continuing treatment with a personally chosen team, the sometimes elusive "life worth living" is emerging. We continue our work with NAMI, www.nami.org, and now with an emphasis on the National Education Alliance for Borderline Personality Disorder, www.borderlinepersonalitydisorder.com.

Through the past ten years of advocacy, I can truthfully say we don't hide, we don't isolate, and we are very vocal about the fact that mental illness IS an illness, that there is treatment and pain can be soothed. Although I still work on guilt issues with my therapist, shame is no longer an issue.

Jim's Story

While on a business trip during a meeting with a customer, I received a call from Diane informing me that our child had just attempted suicide and was being treated in the ER of a nearby hospital. I'll never forget the kindness and understanding of my customers. Both were considerate of my distress and that notwithstanding or perhaps because of these acts of kindness, I, for the first time, felt a sense of shame. What could I have done to cause such horrors to descend upon my child??

At this juncture and after many years of struggle, I developed a sense of the great seriousness of my child's pain. Previously I had adopted the concept that if only more effort was put into looking at the good things in life, that was all that was needed to end the constant trials and tribulations. I had much, much to learn. But, I believed, nothing good was to come of the long and suspicious process of past and continuing therapies and therapists for our child. I was deeply resentful and had an internal fire of anger burning. I carried great conflicts within myself, not understanding the basis or causes for the behaviors with the outward and inward destructiveness combined with my extreme feeling of helplessness of not knowing how to fix what appeared to be an un-repairable situation. Would this ever go away, would it stop? There was no useful knowledge, no skills, and no one to confide in to guide me to help a person whom I loved but whose behaviors I intensely disliked and felt embarrassment for - and even shame.

Years later I learned how I had been focusing on influencing outcomes and truly did not effectively speak the language of validation nor effectively practiced acceptance. I did not have a clear picture of my role in a life affected by a serious mental illness. My former self of being a reactive, volatile parent was a candidate for a serious re-make. I began to learn I would have to develop emotional courage, wisdom and skills which I previously did not have to face the fury of encounters and catastrophes caused by extreme behaviors. The example of airlines instructing us to put on our own oxygen mask and then our child's, became the primary approach in our re-learning role of parenting and care-giving. I first had to deal with me!

My education waited 17 years to begin and it was a NAMI Family to Family course where I leaned the reality of mental illness and how widespread it is. I gained a sense of joy and empowerment as I learned how to deprogram my mind from the hateful stigma of mental illness. Also, I heard the names and several characteristics of many commonly defined mental illnesses which helped me appreciate the extremely high co-occurrence of these illnesses with BPD. Anxiety, depression, eating disorders, substance abuse and other comorbid conditions , all fiercely driven by an over-heated emotion system, unable to be safely regulated.

Only slowly did I learn that the only power to create positive change is when I change myself. This, then, opens the door for others to change. "A change in you means a change in me".

Subsequently, in 2003, Diane and I attended NEA-BPD's second annual conference in White Plains, NY, where we were greeted and treated warmly by an amazing group of clinicians and researchers who had committed themselves to treating and understanding this serious psychiatric disorder that had been shunned by the majority of professionals in the field. They clearly understood the critical and helpful role of families in the recovery process for BPD.

We trained to teach both NAMI's Family to Family 12 week course and

NEA-BPD's Family Connections, 12 week course. One winter, we taught both courses simultaneously. Every teaching experience became more and more therapeutic. We learned more each time and our support system expanded with each class. We started a support group for families with loved ones with BPD and invited BPD informed professionals in Houston to speak and lead discussions. We encouraged class participants to train and teach as well – education and knowledge spread, families began to heal – miraculously including ours!

We've learned that the family needs first to regulate our own behaviors and learn unashamedly to accept our loved ones as they are and ourselves as we are. We have learned that we cannot directly control or change another person and so, we must adopt a willingness to not allow ourselves to ask for something another person cannot presently do. We have to keep in mind always that those with borderline personality disorder are motivated and/or dysregulated by relationships.

Acceptance is the first step "out of Hell" as Dr. Marsha Linehan says. Judgments are an enemy. Without harsh judgments acceptance becomes an easier and better path to follow. Validation is the key to healthy communication and the path to healing misunderstandings. However, it is tricky to only reinforce healthy behaviors, thoughts, and feelings, especially in an emotion-charged and threatening atmosphere. Communication needs to be adjusted to a few words spoken quietly and without excitement and best when all parties are prepared to listen and fully engage. Describe an action as being ineffective rather than bad. Be curious without judgment. During a presentation, a wonderful mental health professional confirmed that communication outcomes are bettered when the family focuses on being clear, calm, consistent, and predictable.

Validation is an extremely important skill for any family and any relationship challenged with emotion dysregulation. An excellent book on the subject has recently been written by Karyn Hall, PhD, and Melissa Cook, LPC, "The Power of Validation". It targets young families with the subtitle of "Arming Your Child Against Bullying, Peer Pressure, Addiction, Self-Harm and Out-of-Control Emotions", but the guidelines pertain to any age group.

It was shocking to learn that even the thought of suicide works for many emotionally dysregulated people in the sense that it offers a calming effect to an out-of-control emotion system. Threats of suicide bring a chilling fear to all who have a loved one they care for. Many of us have submitted to demands we regretted when threatened by the possibility of the ultimate catastrophic loss. With thorough education on the disorder, we've learned that our thoughts of "saving" our loved ones through delivering the demand, may only produce more of the same behavior and perpetuates the cycle of "you fix this – not me".

As I began to educate myself and understand BPD, insights into the disorder began to emerge. We were at a large family gathering one holiday and our adult child was participating, laughing, and interacting and then abruptly left. I followed my child outside and engaged in a supportive conversation when I was tearfully told that the strain of being with all of the family was unbearable even though there had not been a negative incident. The fear of being triggered by an unintended comment was driving this reaction – what a revelation for me!

Families and loved ones would benefit so much more from therapy if the family unit were included as part of the program. I rejoiced when I heard Dr. Marsha Linehan say that she routinely refuses to take on a new patient unless they agree to include family in the program. Does it make sense to intensely treat a client with skills for a better life and then return them to a household or a family unit that is uninformed and unskilled? We need help in recognizing that if what we have been doing to help or control behaviors has not been working, we must try something else!

Our Summary

To sum up our family struggle with guilt and shame, I, Diane, work on the conflict that I willfully believe I did something I should not have done, and on the other side of the coin, Jim faces the realization that he did not parent the way he believes he could have (more validation, less invalidation, more together time). Now, we're dedicated to the willingness that although the "guilt coin" attempts to pop up now and then like a bad penny, we can spend it on making amends with our loved ones, learning and using new skills, being accountable, and helping other people on their similar recovery paths. jh

The How Skills including Willingness and Acceptance in this book are excellent to guide us all through the forest of shame and guilt. Self-blame, Karyn Hall writes, is unhelpful and makes acceptance difficult. It's part of the problem, not part of any solution. The past must be accepted with a move forward and a willingness to focus on current behavior. Be mindful and appreciate today, the present. Now, we know changes can be made, we can learn new skills, and always be willing to try.

Please refer to the How Skills for guidance and affirmation that there are skills for families that contribute very significantly to the recovery process. Therapy, medication, and education all play important roles in the journey but the addition of family skills WILL bring changes in the dynamics of the family circle.

18 Validating Hope: Recovery is Possible

Tami Green

I walked into Dr. Karyn Hall's Dialectical Behavior Therapy Center to begin her Skills Training class about five years ago, newly diagnosed with Borderline Personality Disorder, on the heels of three suicide attempts and a life in utter shambles. Much worse than the financial disasters that I had to dig myself out of were the relationship difficulties I'd created with virtually every person I cared about. My suicide attempts were the behavioral expression of what my emotional state was: dejected and full of overwhelming grief at the pain I'd caused others. I felt the world truly would be a better place without me.

That is where the journey I am describing to you began, but since that very low place, so many miracles have unfolded – more than I could have imagined. Take the fact that I'm writing this chapter, for one. Or that I am able to take my experience with both the suffering and the recovery from this disorder and use it to help others. But the greatest miracles of all center around rebuilding relationships, and that I am daily surrounded by peaceful love.

Before I go on, I want to add a disclaimer here lest you think people have to lose everything to get help. I didn't have to lose everything to get into good treatment, as I'd sought help most of my life. It took me becoming suicidal for the clinical community to finally recognize my symptoms as being BPD. Most everyone I know with BPD has spent a lifetime in therapy, support groups, hospitals, treatment centers, self-help books, etc. looking for help before "hitting bottom". I can't guarantee your adult loved one with BPD will seek treatment or get into the right program. What I have to offer you is my experience as someone who has recovered from the symptoms, and someone who coaches people daily and see them get better, and who also has many friends and colleagues with the disorder who are happy and healthy today.

A few years ago, while still very symptomatic, I testified at a Congressional luncheon, and in doing so, "came out" as one with this disorder and have devoted myself since that time to getting the message out that recovery from the symptoms of BPD is possible. Research shows it.

Every year in recovery offers something new and amazing. This year is a year where I am adding to the focus of my coaching work to reflect what is happening in my own life, in my own recovery. And it is serendipitous that I was asked to write this chapter *now* in my life, for as I write this, my lap-top is resting on top of my very large belly, with an amazing little baby kicking inside – proof of all that is possible in healing relationships and right with the world. My passion is all about others learning that **relationship** recovery is possible, not just disorder recovey. Yours *and* mine.

So, here briefly is how I got from that place, to this place, and hopefully you will be a little inspired in your journey to believe in the good things that await you and that there is hope.

When I first entered treatment, my very weary husband asked our therapist if my "episodes" would ever end. When highly dysregulated, my episodes consisted of suicidal behaviors, drinking, isolating, raging, and texting obsessively. Your loved one may exhibit some of these, all of these, or different ones.

Our therapist laid out what we could expect, and it sustained each of us in very different ways. He said that the episodes would decrease in intensity, duration and frequency over time. So, if the episodes were then once a week, lasting three days, with an intensity level of ten, and thereafter decreasing, so that after six months they may only occur once every other week, last only a day each, and be less intense, for example.

New behaviors are established in DBT by learning them, practicing them, and by testing them. Every week I was learning something new to practice, and added something new to my "tool-kit" of more helpful things to do. Sometimes they would work, but sometimes they didn't for many reasons. Even then I was able to see why they didn't work. Maybe it *was* skillful behavior on my part, but the individual didn't *want* me to succeed, or maybe

I didn't quite have it right yet, or maybe I just needed to be consistent with the new behavior to see more long-term change.

And even when I'd relapse, and just dive headlong into old behaviors that left me and my loved ones traumatized, I was taught how use the unfortunate incident to mine it for clues as to whether or not my thoughts and behaviors were working for me, or to look for vulnerabilities that I could have headed off earlier so that I didn't go there next time.

And, most shocking to me was that I was practicing skills that actually *did* calm my intense emotions.

So, at first we learn to get our ineffective behaviors under control, our intense emotions begin to soften, and we begin to see the cause and effect of our thoughts, feelings and actions. We also practice and build interpersonal skills to more effectively communicate and to accept, understand and validate ourselves and others, just as you are learning here. As we understand ourselves better, we are able to know what we want so that we can set long-term goals, we learn to reward ourselves for small steps towards goals, and we learn to do things daily to increase our feelings of competency.

As this happens, our relationships improve greatly. But with our changes also come unexpected challenges. The balance of power may shift from us being dependent to a more equal partnership, and that may be difficult for our care-takers to navigate. Or we may learn skills while family members are still left trying to communicate with us with old patterns. Old opinions and judgments (and PTSD?) may impede others from seeing our new experience and they may escalate their emotions, bracing for conflict, when there is none. These are some of the unexpected dialectics of recovery I see often, and if you **both** are learning these principles, oh my how quickly things can turn around.

Therapists who are behavioralists believe that we *can* influence others' behavior when *we* change. For example, my role within my family has changed from being the "scape-goat" as I changed my behaviors and now, in turn, I am treated differently. So, I want to reiterate what Karyn (Dr. Hall) said earlier – your relationships can change, *a lot*, even if you are the only one practicing new relationship skills.

Practicing the concept of validation that you are learning here is one such example. When you validate your loved one, you may help to calm their intense emotions, and in doing so, they will be able to have a rational discussion, or are preventing them from yelling. You are effecting their behavior by validating them.

But there is a longer-term effect of validation on someone with Borderline that is extremely powerful in changing him or her that I'd like to describe here. It has been explained to you how invalidation can help set up the disorder in an individual (another example of changing someone with your behavior), and I want to explain what that feels like. Let's use the example of a child who is very, very terrified about leaving his mother on the first day of kindergarten. The child cries inconsolably while the rest of the class goes on with their day. The teacher, exasperated, points out to the child that the rest of the class is fine, and that he is being too emotional and should go sit quietly and do his work like the others.

If I am that young child, and my experience is that I am terrified, and my teacher tells me that my experience is wrong, or I shouldn't have it, or that I should be like the others, (all examples of invalidation), I learn to not trust my own experience, because my experience is wrong. I *am* terrified. That is my experience. But I was told by someone I trust that that should not be my experience. Therefore I learn to disconnect from own inner guidance system that confirms my true self to me. I learn to not trust myself and to look to others to tell me my experience, or to give me direction in problem solving.

It's very hard to describe, this unstable sense of self that is developed in us. But not knowing oneself is also why we "attach" to people and institutions in order to feel stabilized. We are desperate to be understood, as we can't understand our own experience. To add insult to injury, because we walk around in so much pain, and because we have such baffling behaviors as a result, we receive *more* invalidation that most what we are doing seems so irrational to so many.

I want to explain to you how influential you can be in helping build that core sense of self by validating someone. You can help rebuild that inner guidance system without them actually knowing it.

It works like this: I walk into a room upset with you because you bought my sister a bigger present than you bought me. I feel afraid that you love her more than me, so I yell at you, "You love her more than me." A typical response would be, "I do not love her more than you." If I don't really understand myself, and my experience is fear that you don't love me, then you are not helping me connect with my experience. And until I understand my experience, I can't accept your logic, or get better. Since I was taught not to trust my experience, I don't know how to do any of this, and just feel more terrified, hurt and upset by the whole exchange.

For someone skilled at validation, they would look beyond the accusation and look to what my experience was in that scenario and speak to that. The response would be, "you seem afraid that I don't love you as much as your sister." Ah ha. I am feeling afraid. That *is* my experience. And every time we connect with ourselves in that manner, we get a little closer to becoming whole. Eventually it becomes much less important that you understand us, as we "get" ourselves. Big important stuff for parents and kids.

Many of those closest to me where usually invalidating to me in my recovery, but I learned how to rebuild myself by practicing self -validation and using life coaching techniques that I now teach my coaches.

This took me a long time and a lot of work, and is not as quick a turnaround as a behavior change.

For me, learning to be mindful of my loved one's experience divorced me from taking it in as not my own and reacting to it. I learned to just observe, without judgment, and then just describe it back to them. This was HUGE for me, as before I just immediately reacted to what was being expressed

Much has been described about validation in this book, and, though it is a simple concept – put aside your opinions and judgments, observe the person's experience, and describe it back to them – the effects on one's life are profound.

The understanding of dialectics is also enormously healing for us, and we can learn to do it just by hearing you apply it over and over again.

After validation comes the other skills, and radical acceptance is one of my favorites. It didn't feel great, but I had to accept some painful realities such as: some people in the world intend others harm and trust should not be given indiscriminately, there were those in my life who did not want to re-establish a relationship with me and I needed to move on, many of my behaviors did not serve me well, but were making my life worse and I needed to change them, and that my thoughts did not always serve me well and I needed to learn how to challenge them and replace them with more effective thoughts.

I believe many people with Borderline have a great capacity for this type of self-reflection. You may see us often lost in our thoughts, trying to figure things out, we just need the skills and direction to be able to do it well.

Likewise, we are very capable of changing our self-destructive behaviors if taught how and why. So often I was told to do something differently, or make better decisions, etc., but I couldn't figure out HOW to get there. I was just left feeling more and more inadequate. What seemed intuitive for many—just keep your check-book balanced and you won't bounce checks and have return fees – was a mountain for me. But HOW do I do that when I can't remember what I just spent, or when I can't help but overspend when I am suffering so much and am just reaching for relief.?

Or – quit drinking so much and you won't have hangovers, miss work and lose your job and get in a fight with your girlfriend. Well, yes, but then how will I endure the anguish I am feeling in the moment that is too much for a human being to bare alone?

Karyn mentioned that adults in a relationship don't take this kind of instruction well from one another. Modeling the behavior is more often effective, especially when your suggestions make your loved one feel defensive. My family did not have this training, and your loved one is fortunate that you have it. You will benefit as well.

Today my life looks much different than it did. The dysfunctional ways of relating that my husband and I brought into our marriage are being replaced with skillful ways, and we are happily married, my relationships with my children are improving and I feel like I can now be a supportive mother to their needs, I have dedicated my life to helping others (see coaching chapter next) and I am patting my baby bump, a little bundle of miracle that is putting a smile on all our faces. I am peaceful, calm and content.

What remains about me is that I am still a very sensitive individual, though I have many more positive experiences and emotions than negative now. It *hurts* me when I see people being cruel, or insensitive or even dismissive. I *love* deeply and still want to act on the impulse of those feelings by hugging someone, or sending an "I love you" message, but I refrain when it's probably not effective to do so.

If all the world were like me, the "rules" would be different about those sorts of things. But the world is not just like me, and I've learned to accept differences, find that kernel of truth in another's beliefs, understand "why", and soothe myself when I am feeling poorly.

Resources

NEA BPD Family Connections
http://www.borderlinepersonalitydisorder.com/

Treatment Implementation Collaborative www.ticllc.org

Dealing With Emotions www.dealingwithemotions.org

REFERENCES

Brown, B. 2010. *The Gift of Imperfection.* Center City, MN: Hazelton Publishing.

Linehan, M.1993. *Cognitive Behavioral Treatment of Borderline Personality Disorder.* New York: Guilford Press.

Linehan, M. 2011. Workshop, Austin, Tx.

Rumi, Jalal al-Din. 1998. *The Essential Rumi.* Quality Paperback. From "The Essential Rumi", translated by Coleman Barks with John Moyne, 199

ABOUT THE AUTHOR AND CONTRIBUTORS

Karyn Hall, Ph.D.

Dr. Hall has been in private practice for over twenty years and is the founder and President of The DBT Center in Houston, Texas. The Center is a private practice offering both standard and intensive DBT treatment. She focuses on working with treatment resistant depression, trauma, suicidality, self-injury, eating disorders and borderline personality disorder. An expert in Dialectical Behavior Therapy, she is co-author of The Power of Validation (2011). She is the author of Mindfulness Exercises (2013) and The Emotionally Sensitive Person: How to Find Peace When Your Emotions Overwhelm You, scheduled for publication in 2014.

She is on the Board of Directors for NEA BPD and has presented at both the NAMI national conference and state conference. She has presented for NEA BPD and served as a speaker/trainer for both private and public schools on a national level as well as offering numerous workshops. She has served as a consultant for implementation of DBT in residential treatment, private inpatient and for county mental health organizations.

Jim and Diane Hall

Jim and Diane Hall are both board members of the National Education Alliance for Borderline Personaliy Disorder (NEA-BPD). Both received degrees from Ohio University and University of Houston and pursued careers in business management and speech pathology, respectively. Parents of two adult children challenged with symptoms of borderline personality disorder, they have become full time advocates for those with mental illness and their family members.

Both have taught NAMI's Family to Family and now focus on teaching and organizing NEA-BPD's Family Connections program in Texas. They help facilitate three support groups a month for families and friends who have a loved one suffering from symptoms of BPD. Currently they have been learning about the peer movement and how peers in recovery can be trained to become an integral part in the service delivery model.

Tami Green

Tami Green has inspired clinicians and individuals struggling with mental illness and chronic stress with the inspiring story of her journey through suffering to a rich and joyful life. As the nation's first mental health coach, she works with individuals to help them find their true self, builds a plan and skills to help them get there, and sustains the effort needed to reach their dreams. Her coaching certification program accredits individuals and family members so that they, too, might redeem their experiences and help others achieve health and happiness.

Her long list of credentials include Martha Beck Life Coach certification, NAMI Peer-to-Peer and NAMI Connections certification, DBSA Support Leader training, DBT skills training with Behavioral Tech, Harvard Medical School/McLean Hospital Institute for Coaching education, Mentalization Based Therapy Education by Dr. Anthony Bateman and Dr. Peter Fonagy and countless hours of coaching experience and inspirational speaking to large and small groups.

Samantha Bingham

We all come from different backgrounds and may have been raised differently or are of a different gender. None of us have the exact same story. Many of our stories are very similar yes, but the one thing all of us have in common is our uncontrollable emotions.

Throughout my entire recovery I have battled my emotions. No matter what happened in life, it all boiled down to if I reacted or didn't react to that emotion.

My emotions continued to harm me until I realized they are just like waves at the beach--they will continue to come one after the other. If I can distract my mind from the emotion I do not like, then I can experience a different one. Sometimes it's good to ride that wave and feel that emotion at the same time, then allow yourself to have a new emotion.

When I first started this recovery process, I was not able to accept the fact that I had a problem. My alcohol addiction got worse, my self-harm addiction got worse, and my abuse to family members also got worse.

I was 21 years old when I found out I had Borderline Personality Disorder. It took several months to actually get in enough pain to start working on my symptoms. I was then able to start Dialectical Behavioral Therapy (DBT) and get the help I needed.

After a year of DBT, going to support groups, and other 12 step programs, I was able to start leading and chairing all of those groups.

I have taken a year of Dialectical Behavioral Therapy Skills Training and co-facilitate Tami's Green's online DBT class. I have successfully completed the National Alliance for Mental Illness (NAMI) Connections training and facilitate a support group for those with all diagnosis. I am now coaching other people with Borderline Personality Disorder and watching their lives change just the way mine did. This is what is amazing.

Currently I am working at Memorial Hermann Memorial City Hospital as the Team Lead over the business office. I never thought I would be able to successfully hold a job that I love, appreciate, and enjoy! Without skills it would never have been possible for me to hold a leadership position and I am so thankful for DBT!

Amanda Rances Wang
Amanda Wang was featured in the 2010 July/August issue of Scientific American Mind and has been helping others uncover their story through her peer-led support group in New York City. In addition, she also captures her personal battle with borderline personality through her website, thefightwithinus.com.

Amanda publicly speaks of the hope strength and vitality occurring within the BPD community. With an honest and open look into her own struggles, setbacks, and eventual breakthroughs, Amanda pushes forward, challenging herself and others to find the courage to lead and the strength to endure, despite the odds.

Made in the USA
Monee, IL
15 May 2022

96441012R00098